T0381524

The Reverse Thing

Volume XVII

BY: TODD ANDREW ROHRER

iUniverse, Inc.
New York   Bloomington

The Reverse Thing
Volume XVII

iUniverse books may be ordered through booksellers or by contacting:

iUniverse
1663 Liberty Drive
Bloomington, IN 47403
www.iuniverse.com
1-800-Authors (1-800-288-4677)

ISBN: 978-1-4502-3209-8 (sc)
ISBN: 978-1-4502-3210-4 (ebk)

Printed in the United States of America

iUniverse rev. date: 05/07/2010

A man had an accident.

He lost his sense of time and emotional capacity.

This is his seventeenth attempt to communicate since the accident.

Reverse Thing: A method where absolute reverse aspects are applied to a concept so that hidden understandings, illusions or symptoms of alternate perception dimensions are revealed.

3/24/2010 8:28:19 AM – Adaptation is paramount to happiness; aversion to change is the recipe for sorrow. Label's suggest prejudice and in turn encourage control structures. Those who consider all possibilities seldom overlook the obvious. All problems have solutions and some solutions are problems. When you learn from a mistake it becomes a successful mistake. Absolutes tend to be undetected probabilities. Exerting control over others creates suffering; Exerting control over yourself creates understandings. When the cup in the mind is empty understandings will flow in and the larger ships will not get stuck in the shallows. Intelligence is achieved by knowing and increased by questioning what is known. Control freaks will always perpetuate control under the guise of the safety and well being of others. If you follow the directions you will be safe; if you question the directions you will be wise.

Written education neurosis equation:

X = rewards, luxury; popularity; money

Y = Left brain favoring written language, reading, written language, and math

Z = Left brain favored to the extent right brain traits are hindered, silenced or veiled causing neurosis or altered perception.

X + Y = Z

Simply put a reward is given for favoring left brain so as a being learns written education the more they favor left brain the more rewards they get and this leads to a young person being pushed into this unsound state of mind called schizophrenia.

Schizophrenia: a severe psychiatric disorder with symptoms of emotional instability, detachment from reality, and withdrawal into the self.

Another way to look at this equation is people are being punished for favoring right brain traits. This concept of rewarding behavior plays out on the wide spectrum. For example society in general frowns on people that over eat. Even recently some air travel services have actually kicked people off the plane they deemed were too obese. That is in fact a punishment for exhibiting a certain behavior. If a person drives drunk they may get arrested and punished. So rewarding people for proper behavior and punishing them for improper behavior is a form of control. It is no different than rewarding a mouse with food every time the mouse jumps through a hoop and denying the mouse food when they fail to jump through the hoop. The fundamental problem with this form of control is if one is rewarded for a bad behavior then they will become very bad. For example a soldier is in fact rewarded for killing the "enemy" which is other human beings. A soldier that kills many human beings is favored over a soldier who has never killed any human beings in a combat situation. This is also how racism works. A group of beings that see flaws in another group of human beings rewards members of their "click" for exhibiting "bad" behavior towards the target group of humans they are racist or prejudice against. This reward system for exhibiting certain behavior is exactly what the entire society is based on. The labels change but the rewards for exhibiting desired behavior concepts never changes. If one is in a gang, that gang may ask a recruit to do something "bad" and then reward them if they accomplish that deed.

[Genesis 15:1 .... Fear not, Abram: I am thy shield, and thy exceeding great reward.]

This comment is saying do this fear not "ritual" and you will be rewarded exceedingly. Exceedingly means to a usually high degree. For example if a male takes out the garbage for his female mate she may reward him by tolerating him another day. Exceedingly great reward is suggesting something higher than a normal reward. The comment is suggesting something has to take place, the "fear not" ritual, in order for the reward which is exceeding to happen but the unseen reality is why does this fear not ritual have to happen? Another way to look at it is, why doesn't the exceedingly great reward just happen to begin with or why is there this fear not ritual attached to the great reward?

Here are examples of some other reward type suggestions:

[Psalms 37:9 For evildoers shall be cut off: but those that wait upon the LORD, they shall inherit the earth.]
[Psalms 37:11 But the meek shall inherit the earth; and shall delight themselves in the abundance of peace.]
[Proverbs 3:35 The wise shall inherit glory: but shame shall be the promotion of fools.]
[Matthew 5:5 Blessed are the meek: for they shall inherit the earth.]
[Revelation 21:7 He that overcometh shall inherit all things; and I will be his God, and he shall be my son.]
[Genesis 15:1 .... Fear not, Abram: I am thy shield, and thy exceeding great reward.]

Because these texts are codes these comments are all interchangeable. For example:

[Psalms 37:11 But the meek shall inherit [Genesis 15:1 .... exceeding great reward.]
[Revelation 21:7 He that overcometh shall inherit][Genesis 15:1 .... exceeding great reward.]
[He that fear not (overcometh), shall inherit exceeding great reward]

2

[Genesis 15:1 .... Fear not..][Psalms 37:11 ...; and shall delight themselves in the abundance of peace.]

So these comments are suggesting an exceeding (high) reward for overcoming one's fear or fearing not.

[Revelation 21:7 He that overcometh shall inherit all things..] In this comment "all things" denotes a holistic outlook. Everything is included in the set of all things.

This comment is very interesting because it shows the complexity of these texts and the ones that sense time, the scribes, are not pleased with contradictions even though in reality contradictions are indications of paradox, a right brain trait, certainly relative to these texts, and proof the beings that wrote these texts had applied the fear not ritual to a degree and were thinking in paradox.

[Proverbs 3:35 The wise shall inherit glory: but shame shall be the promotion of fools.]

[1 Corinthians 3:18 Let no man deceive himself. If any man among you seemeth to be wise in this world, let him become a fool, that he may be wise.]

So Proverbs 3:35 is saying if you are a fool your reward will be shame and Corinthians 3:18 is saying if you are a fool you may become wise. What this indicates is the complexity aspect in these texts or another way to look at it is, these texts have a "key" and if that key is not understood the texts are not decipherable and the problem with that is the only way to understand that key is to first apply the fear not ritual in one fashion or another. Someone explaining to you the key is not the same as being mindful of what the key is. A male can explain what pregnancy is but a male will never be mindful of what pregnancy is like to experience.

[Proverbs 3:35 The wise shall inherit glory: but shame shall be the promotion of fools.]

Wise: able to make sensible decisions and judgments on the basis of personal knowledge and experience.

Sensible: having or demonstrating sound reason and judgment.

So a wise person is one that is able to reason soundly. Anyone can reason but not everyone can reason soundly. The ability to reason is relative to ones cognitive ability and cognitive ability is relative to the frontal lobe of the brain.

[Proverbs 3:35 The wise shall inherit glory] = Ones with sound cognitive ability inherit sound reasoning and sound judgments and this makes life very manageable and thus one has a glorious life or a life lacking suffering.
[but shame shall be the promotion of fools.]

Fool: somebody considered to lack good sense or judgment.

So the wise have a sound cognitive ability and contrary a fool has unsound cognitive ability.

Cognitive: relating to thought processes; relating to the process of acquiring knowledge by the use of reasoning, intuition, or perception.

The wise have sound thought processes and that relates to their sound cognitive ability and contrary a fool has unsound thought processes and thus unsound cognitive ability. Wisdom and foolishness are relative to thought processes.

[shame shall be the promotion of fools.] = Shame is a key word because shame is relative to thought processes. Simply put a fool is capable of shame and that shame is relative to their thought processes. This means someone that is wise is not capable of shame and that is suggested in this comment:

[Genesis 2:25 And they were both naked, the man and his wife, and were not ashamed.]

Since [shame shall be the promotion of fools.] and Adam and Eve were not ashamed before they ate off the tree of knowledge it means they were in a thought process state called "wise". The complexity is human beings are born with sound thought processes so human beings are born "wise". Another way to look at it is if human beings on average were born with unsound thought processes or cognitive ability problems we would have become extinct a long time ago by default. If you ever hear a human being say "I am ashamed" and being serious about that, it means their thought processes are not sound. When a human being says "You should be ashamed of yourself." and they are serious about that comment it means their processes are not sound and their cognitive ability is unsound. Simply put, shame is a symptom one has faulty thought processes and that is relative to a faulty cognitive ability and so for them to suggest "You should be ashamed" shows they are not making a proper judgment because the wise or the sound minded are never ashamed. So that being is suggesting "you should be ashamed" but in absolute reality if ones thought processes are stable one would be unable to exhibit shame at all therefore the proper comment is "you should not be ashamed." If you are ashamed about anything ever then it is a symptom your

4

thought processes are not stable or normal and so they are unstable and thus abnormal. Shame is relative to emotional state. Shame is essentially relative to fear. A fool tends to treat symptoms of a problem instead of the actual problem. Addressing symptoms is what economics is founded on.

3/25/2010 12:27:55 PM – When you have a cut and it starts healing sometimes it starts itching. You may go to a Doctor and the Doctor may ask how is the cut doing and you will say "It is itching" and the Doctor will say "That is good and a sign the cut is healing well." If you can transpose that exact concept to the end stages that the right brain is attempting to unveil after education has veiled it tends to end with depression or suicidal thoughts so one can see depression and suicidal thoughts are an indication the mind is attempting to restore itself or heal. So depression is just like the itching when a cut is healing, it is a good indication and that means not being depressed means the mind has not yet started to heal or restore itself. So since the education affects the cognitive ability and society essentially all got the education then it means society will see "happy" beings as a good indication of mental health and see depression as a bad indication of mental health. In reality after one gets the education, one senses time, so if one of these beings is happy about their situation they are not very mentally healthy and if they are depressed it means they are attempting to heal or become mentally healthy, restore or heal their mind.

X = one that senses time that appears happy

Y = one that senses time that appears depressed or suicidal

X is very far away from restoring right brain traits and Y is very close to restoring right brain traits and it is logical society would see X state is good and Y state is bad relative to mental health because society has its cognitive ability altered by the written education so its ability to reason is essentially so hindered it is the absolute reverse of reality relative to perception. A scenario would be society would see a depressed person and say we have to give them pills to fix them but that is really saying "They are starting to restore their right brain traits and return to sound mind and our pills will stop that." Simply put society is trying to discourage the ones that are trying to restore their right brain traits, the depressed, and they are encouraging ones that are not at that stage, the happy, to stay away from that stage. So society is saying "If you are depressed or suicidal you need to seek help and take our pills to fix that " but in reality society is saying "If you are depressed you are attempting to mentally heal from the mental damage education caused and you need to seek help and take these pills to stop that." This is all an indication society has had its cognitive ability which is relative to reasoning, perception, and intuition altered as children as a side effect of learning the written education at such a young age. One way to look at it is society or the ones that sense time, the scribes, make decisions but they are not reasonable or cognitive decisions they are unsound decisions and unreasonable decisions. They are not able to reason in that state of mind and that is logical since they are in an altered sense of time perception dimension.

3/27/2010 8:14:07 PM – This is relative to this control mentality that is caused by being in the extreme left brain state of mind caused by written education.

X = a fresh water source
Y = A controlling aspect of that water source
Z = consumers of that water source

(Y) would be a company or a government or any type of control structure. So once Y assumes control of X they have a monopoly on the resource and so they are in fact controlling something that (Z) requires to live. Another way to look at it is, if I take out a patent on oxygen and from that point on I charge any creature that breathes oxygen a fee per breath I have in fact created the illusion of supply and demand when in reality there is no supply and demand relative to economics.

[Exodus 2:17 And the shepherds came and drove them away: but Moses stood up and helped them, and watered their flock.]

This comment is saying in spirit:"And the control freaks, scribes, came and claimed all the natural resources and then attempted to charge common people and controlled the resources and were prejudice against anyone that attempted to use the natural resources that are the factual property of all beings to begin with" and Moses said "You cannot do that to people on my watch control freak." Now I do not expect a control freak or a being with infinite self esteem issues to grasp that concept but none the less it is a true concept. This control freak mentality is a trait of left brain and so control starts with the monetary system. Simply put if I had enough money I could theoretically buy all the land and all natural resources and all the food and everyone's home and leave everyone to die in the streets and the law itself would defend my right to do that because I had enough money to do that. The problem with money is it gives a person the impression they can do whatever they want as long as they have enough money and that is an illusion. Right now companies are foreclosing on human beings houses and some of those human beings are killing their self to make a statement. The problem with that is since the bullies, the scribes, play the game "Money gives you the right to mistreat people just to get more money" I play the game "I beat bullies to death with my words because it is a natural reflex."

6

When no strategy works, all strategies work. The entire concept of control is nothing but a symptom of a being in the extreme left brain state and it is known in the ancient texts as coveting. The scribes covet the natural resources, covet all the people, covet all the children, covet all the land, covet all the sand, covet money, covet control, covet power and thus covet tyranny. Scribes can pass infinite laws that say I cannot go drink from a body of water because a certain being paid money and owns that water but all that really does is proves scribes are infinitely delusional. Scribes assume money means a human being owns water. When the scribes convince me they are God I will acknowledge their laws are more than stupidity invented by mentally unsound abominations. A control freak will get his way if he can scare you enough to make you conform to his control. If one is fearless a control freak has to kill them in order to control them. Law enforcement is what is supposed to scare you into conforming to the will of a control freak. There are many examples in history of a control structure passing laws that discriminate against people for various reasons and then the "law enforcement" carries out those laws that are discriminatory against those people. If they pass a law that says "Anyone that does not follow the law will be killed" law enforcement will go out and kill anyone that does not follow the law and that means law enforcement is a mindless drone. Law enforcement will kill innocent beings if they are told to and they will not question that ever, so law enforcement is simply the hammer wielded by a control structure. A person signs up for a job and suggests "I will do anything you suggest I do" and that is what law enforcement is. If the control structure passes a law that says "kill anyone that talks bad about the control structure" law enforcement will do it, and if that is children or old ladies it makes no difference whatsoever. I will put it to you this way. The control structure says "Anyone that does not give the children our "brand" of education is a threat to that child and they will be punished if they resist's giving that child our "brand' of education." and so law enforcement will lock a parent in jail if any parent resists giving their child that "brand" education.

http://finehomeschooling.com/homeschooling-laws.html

"Every state has some form of a compulsory attendance law that requires children in a certain age range to spend a specific amount of time being educated.'

[attendance law that requires children in a certain age range to spend a specific amount of time being educated.] = Every child by law must be taught reading writing and math and the exact same beings that passed that law are no longer at the mental capacity to even grasp all those left brain favoring education tools affect the mind of a child, that's mind does not even mature until they are twenty. Relative to law enforcement if any parent attempts to keep that education away from their child they will be locked in jail and their child will be taken from them and the law enforcement will say "We are just doing our job." The law enforcement, soldiers, that nailed Jesus to the cross said "We are just doing our job." Simply put all that left brain favoring education veils the right brain intuition so a being is no longer able to think for their self so they become a sheep and thus become mindless specters that are no longer able to even make elementary logical decisions because if they attempt that they may become outcasts relative to their peer acceptance, and so they end up doing things just to be accepted. You can look at a gang and see that lower members in the gang may do things they are not pleased to do just so they will be accepted by higher ranking gang members. That exact same concept is what civilization is.

"Only a short time after compulsory attendance laws became common in the United States, Oregon adopted a statute outlawing private schools which the U.S. Supreme Court subsequently struck down as unconstitutional in its 1925 ruling in Pierce v. Society of Sisters of the Holy Names of Jesus and Mary, 268 U.S. 510 (1925)."

[compulsory attendance laws] Essentially one has to start school at age six or seven and must attend until they are sixteen at least in every single state in America and that means if one attempts to avoid that they are a criminal.

Y = "In humans, the frontal lobe reaches full maturity around only after the 20s, marking the cognitive maturity associated with adulthood" - Giedd, Jay N. (october 1999). "Brain Development during childhood and adolescence: a longitudinal MRI study". Nature neuroscience 2 (10): 861-863.

Z = " If you reflect back upon our own educational training, we have been traditionally taught to master the 3 R's: reading, writing and arithmetic -- the domain and strength of the left brain" -The Pitek Group, LLC. ,Michael P. Pitek, III

Z + Y = mentally hindered

Every single state in the country I live in believes: Z factored in with the reality of Y means children of six years of age will not be mentally harmed so clearly the country I live in has on a whole does not have the cognitive ability to understand obvious cause and effect relationships. That's unfortunate. Another way to look at it is, the vast majority of people in the country I live in are so factually insane and thus not able to achieve basic cognitive abilities that they have created laws and support laws that suggest it is compulsory to mentally damage every single child in said country. Every single being in the country I live in agrees with a law that says "Make sure you mentally hinder every single child starting at the age of six and if you resist you will be punished and labeled a criminal." Another way to look at it is this.

You have heard the story of David and Goliath. You have it in your mind, there is this little defenseless being facing this huge giant with vast armies. It is along the lines of being outnumbered six billion to one and the six billion have all the weapons and you have some crap sling shot. There are only a few human beings in all of recorded history that could stand up to Goliath. And by recorded history I am not talking about 2000 years which is the scribes delusional account of recorded history I am talking about 5400 which is actual recorded history because that is when we invented written language that enabled us to record history. The main reason civilization uses 2000 years to define history is because that just so happens to be in the time frame one human being woke up very well from the written education induced neurosis and achieved a level of explaining the situation relative to the damage cause by the written education flawlessly and the scribes, the ones that sense time butchered him and so they are pleased to remind every other being what happens to beings that wakes up from the neurosis and attempt to wake the others, knowingly or unknowingly.

[Mark 11:18 And the scribes and chief priests heard it, and sought how they might destroy him: for they feared him, because all the people was astonished at his doctrine.]

[And the scribes ..., .. sought how they might destroy him]

3/28/2010 12:30:52 AM – When right brain is unveiled one wins by losing; that reality is completely against the norms of the ones that sense time, the scribes, and also clearly shows the flaws in the language. I go into chat rooms and suggest my comments and then I get attacked and mocked and spit on and then I ponder exactly what triggered that with right brain pattern detection and then I adapt and try again. Another way to look at it is, the hotter the coals are the better I get. This means right brain prefers impossibility because impossibility is the absolute way to get better the fastest. This means I am not as much concerned about saying the right thing as I am concerned about getting the most data from each experiment in the chat rooms. So the flaw in the language is although I lose relative to convincing the ones that sense time to apply the remedy or even convince them to understand education has unwanted mental wide effects I get better from those understandings so I win, and so the ones that sense time become nothing but a mechanism to experiment with by suggesting ideas to better myself. Because pattern detection is the key to coming to further understandings one has to seek the hot coals in order to detect patterns. This is in part why the disciples were slaughtered among others. They were experimenting in the crowds of people with their "doctrine" attempting to improve their ability to explain it and eventually the ones that sense time had enough of their experimenting and killed them. This means I do not get better by talking to ones who have applied the remedy because they are agreeable or we are in agreement so I have to talk with ones that disagree and the more

9

they disagree the better. Society, the scribes are all about "doing it right the first time" as if they even know what that means. That "doing it right the first time" concept is contrary to how a sound mind works. This is complex because economics is based on doing it right the first time and that is relative to efficiency.

Efficiency: the ability to do something well or achieve a desired result without wasted energy or effort.

[without wasted energy] This word wasted is a fear tactic word. The ones that sense time will suggest "Don't waste your life" and at the exact same time they will veil the child's right brain so that child will be nothing but a mental waste. Essentially the ones that sense time do not even know what their own words mean. In the machine state the mind is unable to determine what wasted energy is at all. This means it cannot tell when it is losing or when it is winning so it never gets to the perception of waste. I may be factually wasting my energy attempting to communicate with beings that have been conditioned into an alternate sense of time perception dimension but my mind does not detect waste so relative to my perception I just do, and I am not stressed out or afraid of wasted energy. So the concept of wasted energy is relative to money or economics.

[the ability to do something well or achieve a desired result] This comment suggests an ending or a closure. The ones in the sense of time dimension are all about endings and closure and that is logical because in the no sense of time perception dimension there is no ending and no beginning so no closure, there is only seeking and understanding in order to seek another understanding into infinity. In an infinite loop achievement is not possible and thus [achieve a desired result] is not relevant. What you are detecting is the complete disconnect between the two perception dimensions. For example ones that sense time look at death as an end and ones with no sense of time look at death as another understanding or concept. So in the sense of time perception dimension death is ominous; an ending and closure and in the no sense of time dimension death is a concept that is no different than any other concept. Simply put there is no prejudice in the no sense of time dimension and there is only prejudice in the sense of time dimension. I would never be afraid to listen to a song or to music because I may come across something to ponder and in turn may come to further understandings so I am not prejudice against any music but in the sense of time dimension beings dislike certain music and assume it is because they have a taste in music but in reality they are based on prejudice which is saying they are in extreme left brain state and they see many parts. This seeing parts or prejudice aspect eliminates or silences probability and so a human being is robbed of potential because they only see parts which are absolutes.

Probability: something that is likely to happen or exist.

Absolute: completely unequivocal and not capable of being viewed as partial or relative.

Probability is relative to ambiguity a right brain trait and absolutism is relative to parts a left brain trait and also tyranny. A law itself is absolutism and thus a form of tyranny. No one is above the law which is a nice way to say all laws are absolute. The minute a person subscribes to a law or a rule they lose their objectivity.

[compulsory attendance law] relative to education means we lost our objectivity relative to education methods so we are screwed as a result. Simply put if this attendance law was never created it is possible some parents would have given their children strictly oral education and then it would have been understood they were better off and then someone would ask "What kind of education did you give your child?" and they would have said "Strictly oral education." And then we would have pondered that and perhaps experimented with oral education as another form of educating children. But that is not the case because this compulsory attendance law created in eliminated the probability that scenario would ever happen.

[compulsory attendance law] This means the scribes are absolutely certain beyond life itself there are factually no problems at all relative to teaching all the sequential based education, reading, writing and math, to children starting at the age of seven. Simply put I was one of the children that fell under this umbrella [compulsory attendance law]. Apparently at this stage I am just explaining to you the definitions of words. I have determined you shall be taught the definitions of words.

Another definition of absolute is: having total power and authority. The concept of no one is above the law is fantastic as long as factually mentally unsound lunatics are not making the laws because if that is the case then all the laws are unsound because they are created by lunatics that are mentally unsound. It can be best explained perhaps in an equation.

X = mentally unsound being that has no cognitive ability.
Y = laws
Z = cognitive levels in the laws.

$$X + Y = Z$$

A being that has no cognitive ability will perceive they are passing laws that are reasonable or sound when in reality they are unreasonable and unsound. That is logical because a being that has no cognitive ability is only capable of insanity or stupidity. Stupidity relative to a being that has no cognitive ability is wisdom. A being with no cognitive ability will pass laws they perceive are wise when in reality the laws are stupid.

Stupid : regarded as showing a lack of intelligence, perception, or common sense.

For example: Is passing a law making it compulsory for a child of six to have all that left brain favoring education pushed on them when the reality that their frontal lobe which is relative to cognitive ability does not even develop fully until they are twenty or twenty five a stupid law or a reasonable and intelligent law?

This: [compulsory attendance law] is either reasonable and intelligent or stupid but it factually cannot be both. Another way to look at it is if you perceive this [compulsory attendance law] is reasonable and intelligent then you are factually stupid. You are not factually stupid because that is how you were born, you are factually stupid because you got this [compulsory attendance law]. So that means beings that are all dead now, created this law : [compulsory attendance law] in the early 1870's and now you are stupid as a result of it of course it goes back even to the 1670's but you are confused enough. This is why laws are very dangerous. "No one is above the law" + [compulsory attendance law] is why you are stupid. Someone passed this law: [compulsory attendance law] that said you are going to be made stupid and now you are stupid and that is why no one is above the law. Law enforcement is stupid because they enforce this law [compulsory attendance law] and that ensures they are stupid and that ensures their own children are stupid because they do not think for their self. Government officials are stupid because they allow this law [compulsory attendance law] and that is why they are stupid and that is why their children are stupid and that is why their children will make sure their children are stupid. You do not know what the definition of stupid is so we have to go over that again.

Stupid : regarded as showing a lack of intelligence, perception, or common sense.

Cognition: the mental faculty or process of acquiring knowledge by the use of reasoning, intuition, or perception.

Intelligence: the ability to learn facts and skills and apply them, especially when this ability is highly developed.

Reasoning: the use of logical thinking in order to find results or draw conclusions

Logical: based on facts, clear rational thought, and sensible reasoning.

We have to go through it slowly because you are stupid and the proof is this : [compulsory attendance law] .

[lack of intelligence] is when [the ability to learn facts and skills and apply them] is not developed. You can just insert your name after [lack of intelligence] and that would work also. For example:

[lack of intelligence](your name here)

Let's look at the patterns in the definitions of these words.

Stupid: lack of perception.

Cognition: acquiring knowledge by use of perception.

Intelligence: ability to learn facts = [acquiring knowledge by use of perception]

Reasoning: the use of logical thinking in order to find results = [ability to learn facts] = [acquiring knowledge by use of perception]

Logical: based on facts, clear rational thought, and sensible reasoning = [the use of logical thinking in order to find results] = [ability to learn facts] = [acquiring knowledge by use of perception]

Now, these are patterns that emerge from those patterns.

[sensible reasoning] = [the use of logical thinking in order to find results] = [ability to learn facts] = [acquiring knowledge by use of perception]

Sensible is relative to the senses: having or demonstrating sound reason and judgment.

Perception is a sense. Intuition is a sense and pattern detection is a sense so perception is relative to intuition and also pattern detection and also ambiguity. Ambiguity is a sense.

Ambiguity: a situation in which something can be understood in more than one way and it is not clear which meaning is intended.

For example:

Being recognized by an important being is a treasure beyond value.

One with no ambiguity may determine that comment is saying "Being" as in [the state of existing] and not notice it really is suggesting "Being" as in [a human individual]. So instead of getting one concept from that statement one can get several concepts from that statement that are totally different.

Simply put after all that left brain favoring education the mind loses very important senses called right brain pattern detection, ambiguity and intuition and after that is done the show is over. If you will give up those mental aspects for the promise of money or for the acceptance for your peers or to follow the law then you will kill small children for folly.

Folly: a thoughtless or reckless act or idea.

This [compulsory attendance law] is this [a thoughtless or reckless act or idea.] and that law is a symptom of this [lack of perception.] and that is caused by this [reading, writing and arithmetic -- the domain and strength of the left brain] and that allows this [compulsory attendance law]. It is a perfect infinite loop of destruction. Said infinite loop of destruction is what our species is caught in. I will now ponder why I never will try. - 1:56:13 AM

3/28/2010 3:49:52 AM – In the no sense of time perception dimension one is in the now so they can only learn by making mistakes so in that respect a mistake is not a bad thing at all, it is in fact a concept that is a method to achieve greater understanding. That is completely contrary to the sense of time perception dimensions take on a mistake, the scribes dimension.

Mistake: an incorrect, unwise, or unfortunate act or decision caused by bad judgment or a lack of information or care.

You may have experienced a situation where perhaps a boss at a job or even a parent may say "If you make that mistake again you are in trouble." Society thinks a mistake is an unwise decision or act but right brain learns from making mistakes because right brain is not prejudice so it does not see a mistake as unwise because it comes to further understandings from making "mistakes". So now you perhaps can understand what this comment means:

"What it comes down to is that modern society discriminates against the right hemisphere."
- Roger Sperry (1973) Neurobiologist and Nobel Lauriat

If one is punished for making "mistakes" yet right brain learns best from making mistakes then society punishes people that exhibit right brain traits. For example this is not a mistake: [compulsory attendance law], it is a symptom of insanity. The school system punishes children for making mistakes, misspelling a word, and then that child goes home and is punished by their parents and then that child no longer wants to ever make a mistake so they mentally shut down completely and keep their mouth shut and live the rest of their life in this mental freeze because they know if they make a "mistake" they will be punished. That is a nice way of saying if the scribes are not monsters there are no monsters.

X = The person
Y = Reward for making "wise decisions"
Z = Punishment for making "mistakes"
A = intelligence relative to societies scale
B = Stupidity relative to societies scale

X + Y = A

X + Z = B

The fundamental flaw in this "mistake" or "wise decision" judgment is right brain does not know the difference between a mistake and a wise decision because both lead to further understandings and so both increase understanding and thus intelligence. If you go through life attempting to not make "mistakes" your potential intelligence will suffer because there is no such thing as a mistake there is only further understandings which lead to further intelligence into infinity. The entire control structure relative to civilization is so flawed elementary logic is frowned upon and that is a symptom of the neurosis caused by the education. Making a mistake in not a symptom of stupidity because it may lead to further understandings and thus may increase intelligence. There is a concept called "Nobody is perfect", what that really means is intelligence is not relative to mistakes or wise decisions but the willingness to experiment with both to gain understandings. There is a comment attributed to Buddha that says "A bucket fills one drop at a time." This "drop" is an understanding and so it is not a mistake or a wise decision that fills the bucket, the mind, but it is understandings. What that means is a human being with a sound mind meaning right brain and left brain in harmony, and the indication of that is one is mindfully unable to sense time, has the potential for unlimited intelligence. Buddha explained this in a story and the story was something along the lines of, he picked up a handful of leaves and told his disciples the leaves in my hand are what I have told you and the leaves in the forest behind me are what I have not told you. It sounds very egotistical to a person with an ego but the truth is a being with a sound mind or in the machine state can take anything relative to comments or ideas or concepts and go on for infinity combing wisdom out of them and in turn becoming more intelligent and more intelligent. We are so intelligent as beings the very fact we are violent towards each other at all proves something is seriously wrong with our minds. The scribes told you that your intelligence is relative to your genes and my only purpose in life is to convince you they are the greatest liars in the universe. The tribes that still live in the wild and have no education relative to society's education are so intelligent every single thing you can think of to attempt to convince yourself they are not intelligent only will prove how intelligent they are. Firstly they do not push left brain favoring education on their children so right off the bat they are infinitely more intelligent that all of civilization combined. They have infinitely more foresight than all of civilization combined and they make infinitely more intelligent decisions than all of civilization combined and the harshest reality I have to face is they think I am associated with society so they want nothing to do with me. One aspect that you will certainly comment on relative to the tribes is that they do not have medicine like society does so that proves they are not intelligent. Look at this comment made by Einstein.

"Einstein refused surgery, saying: "I want to go when I want. It is tasteless to prolong life artificially. I have done my share, it is time to go. I will do it elegantly." - Cohen, J.R.; Graver, L.M. (November 1995). "The ruptured abdominal aortic aneurysm of Albert Einstein". Surgery, Gynecology & Obstetrics 170 (5): 455–8. ISSN 0039-6087

[It is tasteless to prolong life artificially].

Tasteless: showing a lack of taste or judgment in aesthetic or social matters.

What you do not see is that this extreme left brain state has made our species afraid or everything and death is what we are most afraid of and so we invent all this medicine to prolong life artificially. People do not prolong life because they are comfortable with death, is another way to look at it. The tribes do not seek to prolong life artificially and that is why medicine does not concern them because sound minded human beings understand if everyone prolongs life artificially the planet will become overpopulated and the entire eco system will collapse eventually. Simply put all that left brain education has given the scribes such an ego and such great fear they are afraid to die and so everything they do in life is relative to fear of death and so they are never at peace. It is quite simple, the ones that sense time that are depressed and suicidal are attempting to make peace with death because they can no longer stand the suffering in that extreme left brain state of mind any longer.

[I will do it elegantly] Only a being of sound mind and thus a being with no ego and no pride would accept natural death when they could prolong their life and that is what elegantly means and that is what grace means. Grace means Einstein had every reason in the universe to not die but he applied self control and saw himself as a part of the system of life and not as the center of the system of life. The disciples did not have to go into those cities when they knew they would be butchered but they did it because they had grace and elegance in the face of madness. Do you understand a being of sound mind must apply self control to be violent towards their own species? Do you understand a being of unsound mind must apply self control to not be violent towards their own species? Do you know prolonging life artificially is in fact being violent towards your own species? Do you understand the tribes that still live in nature do not have prolonging life medicine because they have no aversion to facing death elegantly when it comes because they are not violent towards their own species? Do you understand society has an aversion to facing death elegantly when it comes because they are violent towards their own species? Why do you want to be here any longer than you have to? Do you understand prolonging your life artificially is in fact robbing a younger member of the species of resources? I am mindful if Einstein and the tribes that still live in nature are willing to elegantly let nature take its course then there is no possible logical reason you should not be doing the same. Perhaps we should all go down to the sea shore and attempt to stop the tides from coming in. Perhaps we should dedicate our entire existence to making sure the ocean tides do not come in. In the no sense of time perception dimension the mind is unable to judge death so it is looked at like a concept and in the sense of time perception dimension death is some emotional time based nightmare. News programs thrive on death and make millions of dollars telling you about death because you eat that kind of stuff up because death scares you to death. The sense of time perception dimension makes one reacts adversely to reality because it is an alternate state of reality.

Alternate: different from and serving, or able to serve, as a substitute for something else.

Simply put, all that left brain education has substituted your reality based perception for another perception dimension and thus you have an aversion to reality. If you found out you had cancer would you tell your doctor this "I have done my share, it is time to go." I am mindful all of society would attempt to "save " you and if you resisted they would perhaps force you to seek treatment because they are all essentially have an aversion to reality. They want to save everyone but they do not even have the mental cognitive skills to grasp education hinders the mind because the same education hindered their mind. You are factually not getting out of this place alive and you have an aversion to that and thus you are suffering because you have to go eventually. I look at death as a prime opportunity to distance myself from these poorly disguised thick pamphlet diaries. - 5:27:36 AM

3/28/2010 5:21:26 PM – Laws and rules are secondary to thinking for yourself in all instances.

X = left brain traits
Y = right brain traits
Z = the self

X + Y = Z

When X and Y are in perfect harmony it creates a third being called the spirit and that is what the trinity aspect is. As long as X and Y are in perfect harmony meaning inputs from both aspects are equal the Z or self is in the spirit or the trinity state. The education favors the left brain traits and this diminishes the right brain traits and thus the self is thrown out of the spirit or trinity state. So one has left brain traits and they are contrary to right brain traits but when both are in perfect harmony they create a third trait which is the Holy Spirit. When either aspect left or right is out of sync the Holy Spirit aspect cannot be achieved. So this tree of knowledge sins against the Holy Spirit because in favoring the left brain it destroys the possibility of this trinity or third self aspect so the remedy must be applied to restore the Holy Spirit. Holy relative to this concept is perfect spirit meaning sound minded.

X = all the left brain traits

Y = all the right brain traits

When X and Y are in perfect harmony, for example when linear thoughts are exactly equal to random access thoughts of right brain there is a third mind trait that is created, it could be looked at as a whole mind trait. So the whole mind trait is not left brain or right brain traits it is something in the middle of the two.

A right brain trait is complexity and a left brain trait is linear or simple minded aspects so in perfect mental harmony there is a trait that would be defined as complex simple thoughts. This whole mind aspect is not cut and dry like it would seem. One is not really thinking with one aspect of their mind and then thinking with the other aspect but this whole mind state enables one to achieve both aspects. The simple fact a person with a sense of time can read a sentence and notice "mistakes" in grammar proves they are very focused on details a left brain trait. An English teach sits there all day long and reads what the students write in their papers and they are really just focusing on left brain traits attempting to notice all the details, "grammar mistakes" so they are in fact mentally conditioning their self to favor

18

left brain. The old comment "reading is fundamental" is a fact, but it is a fundamental way of favoring left brain and in turn veiling right brain traits. Reading is in fact a drug that favors left brain traits and combined with the fact a child's mind is developing until they are twenty; it is a detrimental drug to that child's mind. Society as a whole mocks anyone that cannot read; the conclusion is the sooner one can read the better and that also is a death sentence relative to the harmony in the mind. Simply put there is nothing in the universe that destroys a child's mental harmony more than reading, writing and math because that child's mind at the age of seven is very delicate and very sensitive to even the slightest left or right brain favoring conditioning. This is why oral education on an absolute scale is the only safe route when educating children at that young of an age.

The story about Oskar Schindler is a story about a human being that decided to think for himself even though in doing that he was "breaking the law". Right now in society it is against the law to not push the reading, writing and math on children starting at the age of six so if you attempt to avoid that you will be labeled a criminal. This is why thinking for your self is more important than following the law because laws can be flawed. The law relative to education factually is saying "It is against the law not to mentally hinder children or mentally hinder your own child starting at the age of six." whether the law makers know it or not, so you have to make a choice. If the law trumps what you understand is proper then you are less important than an inanimate object which is what the law is, so you have serious self esteem issues. In Schindler's situation it was against the law to not discriminate against certain people and so Oskar decided to become a criminal. When the law says "harm people" and you do not, you think for yourself and become a criminal. This means the word criminal is simply a fear tactic word. If nothing else I am certainly a grammatical criminal but that is just a label. You can call me anything you wish but those labels are nothing but labels. They do not work on me. You can suggest I am the devil himself for giving my testimony relative to what I understand traditional education does to the mind and did to my mind but I am still going to give my testimony. It is not logical I am writing for fame and money when I fully understand if I get good at explaining the damage written education and math has on the mind I will very likely be harmed. All the others that became good at explaining this doctrine were butchered so the very fact I continue to write proves I do not fear death. My mind will not allow fear to get in the way of my purpose and what that means is my hypothalamus no longer gives me fight or flight signals even in the face of literal death potential.

3/29/2010 9:15:58 AM – If you try to reduce everything down to one core symptom of all the left brain education it would be fear. Fear is relative to the hypothalamus and in turn fear is relative to pride and in turn pride is relative to ego. In a scenario where you find yourself in the basement of an abandoned house in the middle of the words and there are no lights and it is midnight and you hear boards creaking upstairs and your mind is telling you to run like the wind the only reason you would not run is if you were completely absent of ego and pride. Think about a war scenario, a guy is in a foxhole and a grenade comes into the fox hole and he jumps on it to save his buddies. A being could not do that if they had ego and pride so at that very moment that being jumped on that grenade they saw their self as nothing or of having no value and so they applied the remedy and if that grenade did not kill them they would unveil right brain to a degree perhaps. Simply put in jumping on that grenade that person feared not or denied their self, self being ego and pride or they submitted. Of course the remedy means one seeks that situation willingly or of free will. To submit is in fact to deny ego and pride. This remedy is not a lifelong profession it is in fact a one second mental exercise to knock that hypothalamus back into working order after the education has put it in a state of sending out far too many fight or flight signals. So in the process of all that left brain favoring education the hypothalamus is effected and so in turn with all the false fight or flight signals the right brain aspects cannot come to the surface so said traits are reduced to a subconscious state and so one is stuck with linear simple minded thoughts and that relative to their perception is a sound mind when in reality that is a devastatingly hindered mind. Another way to look at it is one's mind is so hindered they cannot even tell it is hindered. The mind is so hindered it cannot reach a level to detect it is hindered so in turn it cannot figure out a way to negate the hindering. It is easier to look at it like the education pushed on the mind at such a young age is catastrophic. Complete collapse of the mind to the point the mind does not have the ability to get itself back in order. This is why this written education is a species wide situation and there is no country that has it under control or even has a grasp that it is happening. Civilization perceives the highest IQ a person can have is around 205. That is laughable because with right brain unveiled one can only get smarter and smarter into infinity and on a scale of progression relative to days. This means the a person applies this remedy the full measure and right brain restores after about thirty days and in the following year or so they will understand more than they have understood and their entire life up to that point. You go find a person with an IQ of 205 and ask them what the tree of knowledge is and what its implications are on the species and when they say "I have no idea" and you will understand an IQ of 205 is an indication of mental retardation and nothing more. Because of what this education does to the mind the entire species has a major self esteem issues. The species entire scale of what is intelligence is wrong. I am at a stage where I ponder what kind of grief I want to approach next. Do I want to look any further into neurology because the last time I did I found out because education hinders the right brain and thus right brain intuition it makes it so human beings lose what is called their conscience and what the ancient texts call their soul. Perhaps I will ponder more of these psychological symptoms so I can understand more thoroughly nearly every single psychological disorder essentially is nothing but symptoms the right brain is veiled. I already am fully aware every single person that kills their self because of depression is simply a human being that has right brain random access thoughts absent from their thought processes and if they did not have the random access thoughts absent and they never would have been able to achieve a mindset of depression and thus they never would have achieved a mindset of suicidal thoughts so they never would have killed their self. So with right brain unveiled my problem is not lack of intelligence it is really being concerned about the fact whenever I look into a topic no matter what topic I come to further understandings and the grief increases. You may get the impression with all this mental ability I will solve the world's problems but what you do not understand perhaps is I want nothing to do with society or civilization, the scribes, and the last thing in this universe I want is for society to think I am anything but its adversary on every single level possible. Simply put at the end of the day they are going to continue to mentally hinder the children and so I spit blood on all of civilization. It's not important if you are not pleased with that because you do not have the brain function of a gnat in your current sense of time state of mind. I have to go out of my way to make sure civilization and society never ever gets the impression I am one of them. That is all I need is for civilization to assume I am anything but its absolute adversary on every level of the word adversary.

Adversary: an opponent in a conflict, contest, or debate.

Civilizations debate is, pushing left brain favoring education on children at the age of six is the wisest thing in the universe and my debate is, you might as well just kill the children if you are going to do that so I won't have to write in my books you are a cold hearted ruthless insane cruel bastard like I just did. If civilization ever suggests I am anything but the strongest adversary they have ever faced I have failed. If civilization ever suggests "Look how wise our education has made this being" I have failed. Simply put I am the adversary. I listen to beings that suggest they are "awake" and I hear them on talk shows and they are asked to explain the situation and they say everything in the universe but what is on their mind. They beat around the bush because they are afraid because they did not apply the remedy to the full measure so they are trapped with an ego and with pride. They did not quite understand what the story of Jonah is suggesting. This is where they are at:

[Jonah 1:2 Arise, go to Nineveh, that great city, and cry against it; for their wickedness is come up before me.]

[Jonah 1:3 But Jonah rose up to flee unto Tarshish from the presence of the LORD, and went down to Joppa; and he found a ship going to Tarshish: so he paid the fare thereof, and went down into it, to go with them unto Tarshish from the presence of the LORD.]

They are asked on the talk shows what their understandings are and they are right here [But Jonah rose up to flee]. They have said everything properly so the talk shows invite them on and then the entire world is looking at them and the world says "Tell us what you understand" and they flee like scared dogs and say everything but what is on their mind because they know if they come out and say "written education and math ruins the mind" they will be reduced to the laughing stock and will be mocked and spit on and their little cult following will be reduced to a flock of one and only a being with no ego and no pride would be indifferent to that reality. You cannot make a living in a lunatic asylum.

Where you want to be is here ego wise:

[Jonah 1:12 And he said unto them, Take me up, and cast me forth into the sea; so shall the sea be calm unto you: for I know that for my sake this great tempest is upon you.]

[Take me up, and cast me forth into the sea] Take me and cast me in to the sea I am nothing and I have no value I am zero I have no worth. When you are there you will not be afraid of anything or anyone ever. You will give your testimony and the thought will never enter your mind they may kill you afterwards. Everyone on that boat was scared.

[Jonah 1:10 Then were the men(the ones that sense time, the scribes) exceedingly afraid] and Jonah did the complete opposite of that and said "Not only am I am not afraid in this boat in this storm I beg you to throw me into the sea itself." That is what submission is, that is what deny yourself is, that is what fear not is, and that is what meek is. Of course that is just the remedy and not a lifelong profession. The testimony you give after you apply the remedy and feel how powerful right brain is will be your life long profession and there is no one in the universe that can give your testimony as well as you and if you are worth your salt it will not be that long of a profession so no retirement fund is required. Do you think the scribes are going to appreciate the fact you are telling them written education and math destroyed their minds and they have to mindfully kill their self to return back to where they were as a child mentally? Do you think they are going to say "Thank you for that information I am so pleased with you." Your purpose is to tell the truth and when the scribes mock and spit on you then you will have a nice emotional blocking opportunity so you become better at concentration so the next time you can explain it more boldly. As you explain it better your longevity decreases in this narrow.

[Luke 19:47 And he taught daily in the temple. But the chief priests and the scribes and the chief of the people sought to destroy him,]

This means Jesus was so proficient at explaining the issues relative to the "tree of knowledge" to the common people the ruler scribes had no choice but to kill him. Do you think society is going to show up at your house and give you a medal for explaining flawlessly to the common people the education mentally destroyed them? After you apply the remedy you only have two choices, you either go with the flow or you go hide in a hole and pray for a swift death so you do not have to be mindful of what the scribes are doing to the children.

[the scribes and the chief of the people sought to destroy him,] You are surrounded by six billions scribes so you are either going to hide in a hole or go with the flow but there is no such thing as lukewarm in this narrow. If you even have a drop of fear in you then you need to go apply the remedy to the full measure because sound minded beings are not afraid of anything when it comes down to speaking out against children being mentally harmed on an industrial scale. Six billion scribes are manageable numbers from where I sit. Six billion is not infinity so right brain assures me it must be zero.- 10:38:00 AM

10:49:20 AM –

"For the woman, the man is a means: the end is always the child." - Friedrich Nietzsche

This is a very elementary concept relative to mammals. The pecking order is: the children are the most important thing, the males purpose is to protect the females because the women are the protectors of the children and so males fall in line as a means to accomplish that at the request of the women but also the women attempt to make sure the males do not get to close to the children. Males do not do well raising children because women do well raising children. Now you are thinking in your pinprick mind that this is relative to women having this ball and chain around their foot because their purpose is to raise the children but in reality the children are the only thing that matters and that means adult males do not matter perhaps at all after the reproduction aspect [, the man is a means]. This means the species could perhaps survive without males at all and the species would certainly die without females. Society is complete opposite of reality relative to the way it thinks and that is because they have been mentally pushed into an alternate perception dimension. Are women and children the most valuable or the least valuable relative to society and how society treats them? In reality world where I live they are the most valuable and since I am in reality world it is logical society that has been conditioned into alternate perception dimension would think absolutely contrary to that and they do. Since society is totally backwards the children are least important and the adult males are most important. If society saw any value in the children at all they would be slightly more cautious about pushing all that left brain education on them at the age of seven. The truth is society believes money is more important than the offspring and it shows. I wouldn't have to write infinite book explaining how stupid that education has made you if that education made you wise so that is all the proof you ever need. If you ever want proof just remember I am writing infinite books explaining how stupid that education pushed on you as child has made you. If that hurts your feelings then you need to go take an anger management class because I have not even begun to insult you yet. You better do everything in your power to repeal freedom of speech and freedom of press because if you do not there will be nothing left of your ego when I am finished with you. I am here to destroy your temple and I only think on terms of infinity and death itself is afraid of me. So getting back to the lesson, think about these two comments:

"For the woman, the man is a means: the end is always the child." - Friedrich Nietzsche

[1 Samuel 18:7 And the women answered one another as they played, and said, Saul hath slain his thousands, and David his ten thousands.]

[For the woman, the man is a means] = [Saul hath slain his thousands, and David his ten thousands.] because [the end is always the child.].

[And the women answered one another] This comment is a suggestion of a control structure or a command structure. The women are in control and they gave orders and then men carried them out and they are discussing how well the men carried out their orders [Saul hath slain his thousands, and David his ten thousands.] What orders? Protect the children from the scribes because the scribes are killing the minds of the children by teaching them that tree of knowledge and never suggesting the remedy and thus the children are stuck with pin prick retard minds so kill all the scribes for us Saul and David to protect our offspring because the offspring is the most important thing. That is factual history of mankind and if the scribes suggest to you anything contrary to that remind them I write books attempting to explain how retarded that education has made them and then remind them their best option at this stage of their life is to go mindfully kill their self. That certainly blew it.

Since the scribes are killing the children with the education by hindering their minds then they are killing the species because no species can exist for long with hindered minds so the fact the children are being mentally killed means the species is being killed. The complexity here is the scribes all got the education and did not apply the remedy so they are not even mentally able to grasp that is exactly what they are doing, killing the species. Since they are killing the children they are dooming the species so what does killing even mean? These beings in the ancient texts were the last line of defense to save the species from extinction because they were aware the tree of knowledge, reading, writing and math, was hindering the species mind and no species can survive for long with an unsound mind;

they will destroy their environment and in turn kill their self off. When they find a village with an Ebola outbreak they do not transport them to a populated area and set them free they isolate them and wait for them to die and so they kill them. If you are sick and I do not seek to find you help but instead I isolate you and wait for you to die, I kill you.

[Saul hath slain his thousands, and David his ten thousands.] The men are good at killing and the women are pleased with that prospect. The women are far too busy making sure the offspring are taken care of to bother their self will killing the lunatic scribes so they sent the males out to do the dirty work. Why don't you call your cult leader and ask for your money back because all they have been telling you relative to these ancient texts are lies upon lies upon lies unknowingly. These ancient texts are the only texts in our recorded history that are realistic and the scribers have hijacked them and turned them into an abomination, a joke and a money making opportunity. I saw a show with a politician speaking and he said "We want to make sure all the children get a good education because they are the most important thing." [Matthew 10:16 Behold, I send you forth as sheep in the midst of wolves: be ye therefore wise as serpents, and harmless as doves.]

In your mind you have to be God of War but outwardly you have to be peaceful because you are surrounded by six billion lunatics and they will kill you at the drop of a hat and brag about how wise they are for doing so. This is relative to focusing on the log in your eye. You are not going to be able to stop the scribes from getting all the children. The scribes kill their own children with the education so that means they want everyone to kill their children also because misery loves company. The only thing you can do is apply the remedy and give your testimony because we are far too gone now.

This [Saul hath slain his thousands, and David his ten thousands.] did not stop the scribes thousands of years ago so it is not going to stop the scribes now. In your sense of time perception dimension you do not like situations that do not have beginnings and ends. Left brain does not have the complexity to deal with impossibility and complexity is a right brain trait. You want to win but Saul and David couldn't win against the scribes. Maybe I am out of touch and all of civilization in fact suggests the fear not remedy to the children since they push all that left brain education on them by law starting at the age of seven. The scribes are in another perception dimension completely so when they say we love the children so we educate them all well, it means we kill the children, which is why we educate them all well, and it is as simple as that. How do you propose to reach a being that has been mentally hindered to the point they perceive mentally killing children is mentally loving children? How do you propose to reach a being that has been mentally hindered to the point they mentally damage their own children and then brag about it to their friends and perceive they are wise for doing so? Child protective services will take your child from you if you do not give your child the "brand" of education starting at the age of six. Law enforcement will lock you in jail if you do not give your own child the "brand" of education starting at the age of six. Simply put you attempt to apply the remedy and become a master at concentration so when the education destroys your child's mind you may be at a level of concentration you can assist your child to return to sound mind with the understanding your family members will never believe you and never apply the remedy because somehow that is just the way it is. Buddha went home after he applied the remedy and saw his wife and children and he left because he knew you can't convince the ones you know to apply the remedy. Jesus could never convince his father Joseph and it is understood Joseph did get the curse because he was a carpenter and math is required in the field of carpentry. That is why the tribes that still live in nature do not build permanent houses, because it requires math. One might suggest building the pyramids required math. One might suggest to build a city requires math. One might suggest to charge usury rates requires math. My job would be much easier if all I had to talk about was ghosts, aliens and lizard men.

[be ye therefore wise as serpents, and harmless as doves.] Remember the kingdom is within so mentally you are going to be a leviathan of concentration or you are going to be annihilated by the heightened awareness after you apply the remedy. If you are worth your salt in giving your testimony after you apply the remedy the scribes are going to lock you in jail or worse anyway so there is no reason to show physical wrath. Always remember you have a right to defend yourself and defend the children but not in this narrow.

In many situations relative to mammals the females are in a situation they have to protect the offspring from the males. For example a female lion may have to protect the cubs from a male lion. Ironically the males were the first ones to subscribe to written education and math and the females had to try to protect the offspring from them. So the males invented something and the females realized it was not good for the offspring but the males didn't notice that because they are not in touch with the offspring like the females are. Of course now the females all subscribe to the education so they are ruined until they apply the remedy. Simply put they are not capable of defending the offspring because they are mentally hindered. They are blind to their duty as protectors of the offspring. The females have been put to sleep by the education and because the cohesion of the species relies on the females the males have assumed the leadership role but the males are not the leaders, the females are the aspect that makes sure the offspring are raised properly so the entire network of the species has collapsed. It has nothing to do with morals it has to do with the simple reality that females are good with the offspring and males are essentially worthless outside of the facet they mate with the females, but our species is turned completely backwards and the females are worthless and the males are important. Once the female offspring aspect is hindered the species is hindered is another way to look at it. With this education and economic system we have put the females in a position that they have to decide to either have food to eat by working or raise the children. It is not about females are only capable of raising the offspring it is the fact males are not capable of raising the offspring. I will repeat that since you do not speak English. Males are not capable in any respect of raising the offspring in contrast to the females. A male lion will eat the cubs if the female is not there and that concept applies to our species also. So females are in a situation that society mocks them for doing their job, which is making sure the offspring are raised properly and so the females embrace the education to get a job and in turn forget about raising the offspring. This is all relative to contact. The minute we started putting value on the written education and math we knocked ourselves out of harmony because written education and math are not natural they are manmade and in attempting to fit this man made invention into a natural system the natural system was hindered. The moment the females started getting the education it was all over because they are the cornerstone of the entire system relative to our species. The males can all go jump off a cliff into the sea after they mate with the females and it will not make a dam bit of difference, but once the females started eating off the tree of knowledge we were doomed because they and only they are naturally in tune relative to raising the offspring. Society has convinced the females something is more important than the offspring and the males have encouraged that. Simply put the males are not in control of the species the females are and since this education has thrown us into an alternate perception dimension we have everything backwards. A female has to decide between the offspring and the luxuries of the economic system and that is the position males have put them in and that is why males cannot run the species. We have all these males running around calling the shots and that is that is not how mammals operate. Females, offspring, males is how mammals operate and we have it exactly backwards so we are doomed.

Here is what Mohammed said about females:

"Be good to women; for they are powerless captives (awan) in your households. You took them in God's trust, and legitimated your sexual relations with the Word of God, so come to your senses people, and hear my words ..."

[Be good to women; for they are powerless captives] This is a nice way to say the males ate off the tree of knowledge and went insane and started treating the women as if the women are not the dominate gender and most important gender in the species.

[so come to your senses people] Come to your senses you lunatic males, you cannot have children so obviously you are not worth much because if you cannot have children you cannot raise children. It is very easy to suggest all you have to do is apply the remedy after

27

you get the education and everything will be fine, but the fact is, you call me up after you mindfully kill yourself which is the remedy, and tell me how easy it was. Your optimism is your ignorance. If when you were born you were given all the money and food and shelter you could ever need you wouldn't go to school at all, you would do what your purpose is. So that shows that education is a means to an end; money, food and shelter. That is not a natural created aspect that is a man made created aspect. And all of that is just fine as long as these two realities are lies:

Y = "In humans, the frontal lobe reaches full maturity around only after the 20s, marking the cognitive maturity associated with adulthood" - Giedd, Jay N. (october 1999). "Brain Development during childhood and adolescence: a longitudinal MRI study". Nature neuroscience 2 (10): 861-863.

Z = " If you reflect back upon our own educational training, we have been traditionally taught to master the 3 R's: reading, writing and arithmetic -- the domain and strength of the left brain" -The Pitek Group, LLC. ,Michael P. Pitek, III

If Y and Z are lies everything is fantastic and if Y and Z are true and facts we are screwed beyond your mental ability to even grasp in your big sense of time perception dimension. We have a water supply that is full of a hallucinogenic and we make everyone drink out of it because we are hallucinating from drinking out of it and the only antidote is you have to mindfully kill yourself. I have not convinced anyone to apply the remedy. I just get spit on and mocked. My purpose is to remind you everything you perceive in your entire life that is a problem is nothing but stupidity for fools in contrast to this real problem. So to take it all the way back; Mankind invented written language. It was called by the Greeks Demotic referring to common hieroglyphics which means "popular." In learning this language something called pride and ego are created and in turn right brain traits are veiled because the invention favors left brain and so our ambiguity aspect of right brain was veiled which means we not only were not prone to question if this invention had bad side effects but our pride and ego would not let us question the invention and on top of that the only way to tell if someone has these bad side effects was by their deeds and actions and wisdom or fruits. The damage was not outward it was inward, as in the mind.

"U.S. and coalition forces in Afghanistan have their sights... designed to gain control." – CNN.COM

Control: to exercise power or authority over something such as a business or nation.

Coveting: to have a strong desire to possess something that belongs to somebody else.

[Proverbs 8:36 But he that sinneth against me wrongeth his own soul: all they that hate me love death.] - 5:32:06 PM

3:39:49 PM –

Emotional torment of the minds half spent
Focus on the ground, unutterable words
They aren't deceased; emotional torment with no cure.
Pray for nightmares in your dreams.

Scenes of ones with no doubt
Hurricanes drowned out your shouts
They aren't deceased; emotional torment with no cure.
The trenches they rest in dug long before.
Pray for nightmares to block the door.

Often they pass along the lane
Nightmares that can't complain
Focus on the ground, unutterable words
Pray for nightmares; deny the scourge.

- 3:55:39 PM

3/30/2010 3:12:33 PM –

"The Posse Comitatus Act is a United States federal law (18 U.S.C. § 1385) passed on June 18, 1878, after the end of Reconstruction, with the intention (in concert with the Insurrection Act of 1807) of substantially limiting the powers of the federal government to use the military for law enforcement. The Act prohibits most members of the federal uniformed services (today the Army, Air Force, and State National Guard forces when such are called into federal service) from exercising nominally state law enforcement, police, or peace officer powers that maintain "law and order" on non-federal property (states and their counties and municipal divisions) within the United States. The statute generally prohibits federal military personnel and units of the National Guard under federal authority from acting in a law enforcement capacity within the United States, except where expressly authorized by the Constitution or Congress. The Coast Guard is exempt from the Act during peacetime."

What this is saying is the federal government cannot use its military aspects to enforce laws in a state. As the federal government gets strong and has more influence the state government has less influence and it works both ways. The entire principle of America is that there are fifty odd states and each state is its own separate entity with its own set of laws so the goal of the federal government is to attempt to make each state fall under its umbrella. This Act is supposed to stop that. The problem is in order for the federal government to get around this act all they do is simply train the local police force using its tactics. For example the federal government cannot send marines into a state to enforce laws so what they do is allow that state to carry the same weapons as the marines. These are like swat teams and for example. All a swat team is essentially are [military for law enforcement.] The key to this tactic working is fear. For example each state or city has a swat team and that team is not used often so it is a shady area but not blatant ignoring of this Act but then there has to be home land security and then there has to be "drug enforcement" and all of these aspects also carry military weapons so then this act is being ignored all together on the promise of "safety". Reagan said something along the lines of the government is the problem. This is all relative to control and thus coveting. Left brain loves to control and it controls using fear tactics. "If you say that cuss word you will go to hell." that is as good of a fear tactics as " If you speak out against the government you hate America and you are a terrorist." The problem is George Washington said the government is not reason (insane), so using that logic George Washington was a terrorist and anti- American.

The ones that sense time are in extreme left brain state and left brain loves directions and so this means they love to be told what to do because it gives them a sensation of purpose so the only logical way to proceed is to give them directions. The ones that sense time are seeking directions. Left brain has to be told what to do because it has no right brain intuition. Right brain does not want to be told what to do and also does not want to tell others what to do, it is all about free will so I must apply self control and become a leader that gives directions. I must give directions to the ones that seek directions and I can only do that by applying self control because my nature is to not give directions to anyone but myself. I have to be controlling because my nature is to not control. I have to do something I don't want to do and that requires self control. If I do not give the ones that seek directions a check list of directions then they will not know what to do because they have right brain intuition veiled and thus cannot think for their self. I must give them directions in order to allow them to reach a state they can become their own director and thus the concept, teach them to fish. In order to make a person a fisherman one first has to direct them in the methods of fishing. So I must become a tyrant in order to free them from mental tyranny. Go apply the remedy and then you will have a sound mind and then you can assist others to apply the remedy because you will understand its concepts fully. That was an extremely short lived tyranny. I am mindful to avoid becoming a comedian.

If one attempts to control or manipulate the system called nature they will hinder it. Economics has nothing to do with nature because natural resources are only looked at as money. In an economic system life is not as important as profit. In a control structure what is being controlled is never as important as what is doing the controlling. Everyone is equal until a control structure is introduced. Fear unites the fearful and thus the fearful detest the fearless. The mentally blind cling to safety blindly. Since the mind leads the body if there are no laws to protect the mind the laws to protect the body are fruitless.

My new dog River was outside barking and I walked out and noticed he was barking at the sand and I realized he is a lot like me, and there certainly is a lot of it. Tyrants are pleased with laws that afford them the most control. As the numbers of laws increase freedom decreases and thus fear increases. Even with infinite laws you still will not be safe because you will have fewer options when danger approaches.

2384. Seditious conspiracy

"If two or more persons in any State or Territory, or in any place subject to the jurisdiction of the United States, conspire to overthrow, put down, or to destroy by force the Government of the United States, or to levy war against them, or to oppose by force the authority thereof, or by force to prevent, hinder, or delay the execution of any law of the United States, or by force to seize, take, or possess any property of the United States contrary to the authority thereof, they shall each be fined under this title or imprisoned not more than twenty years, or both."

[If two or more persons]: I am one person that is attempting to [delay the execution of any law of the United States] relative to the compulsory attendance law which means I am suggesting if you are a parent or a being in the United States and you support this brand of education taught to young children at the age of seven while you are aware their frontal lobe does not develop until the age of twenty you are factually less than a human and in fact you are a monster and a threat to yourself and to those around you and you should be locked in a cage until you show signs of cognitive ability. If you follow the compulsory education law you are a mental harmer of children and if you do not follow said law you are a criminal but you can at least be considered in the realm of a human being as opposed to being factually understood to be a mental harmer of innocent children. I know what you are.

I found this comment in the US Child Abuse Prevention and Treatment Act:

In one section is says: Congress finds (1) each year, close to 1,000,000 American children are victims of abuse and neglect;

But the figures are more accurate to this: In the year 2000, there were 76.6 million students enrolled in schools from kindergarten through graduate schools. Simply put the ones that sense time are in neurosis and have their right brain intuition veiled so they are not playing with a full deck of eyes, so to speak. Pattern detection is a sense, intuition is a sense and these right brain traits are veiled by education so one ends up with mentally hindered beings making "laws" with very important senses absent from their perception so in turn their cognitive ability is greatly hindered and thus their "laws" are stupidity or lacking intelligence and foresight.

4/3/2010 12:48:56 AM –

X = food and water and shelter
Y = money
Z = laws and rules
A = punishment for breaking laws
B = necessity
C = "illegal" job
D = "legal" job

$$Y + B + D + Z = X$$

$$Y + B + C + Z = A(X)$$

The problem with the monetary system is food, water and shelter trumps laws and money and civilization and the control structure itself. One is unable to get food and water and shelter unless they have money but the control structure puts limits on how one can get money and the illegal ways to get money and the legal ways to get money are the bottle necks to getting food, water and shelter. A human being will do anything they have to do to get water, food and shelter but the control structure has made it so some of those ways are illegal so human beings are being punished for trying to get food , water and shelter because those "methods" fall outside the limited methods the control structure allows. One can grow their own food but first they need their own land and that requires money. One can drill for their own water but first they need money for a drill. One can build their own house but first they need money to build the house and before that they need money for land and before they do any of that they need quite a bit of money and they will never be able to get that unless they gets lots of education and then they have to get a well paying job. So the control structure creates money and then attaches methods one can earn it but there are limited amounts of ways one can earn it legally. So a criminal is essentially a thief. A thief is simply a human being that is attempting to get food, water and shelter outside of the limited methods the control structure allows. One may hear a police officer suggest to a drug dealer "That is not the way to earn money so now we have to arrest you for earning money the illegal way." A prostitute is a criminal but in reality they are simply attempting to get money so they have food, water and shelter outside the control structures allowed methods. Everything comes back to the education. Get a "good" education and you get money and you can earn money by way of the control structures "legal" methods and if you do not get a "good" education you either get a job that makes you a slave or you become a "criminal". The problem with all of this is money is the method to control people's behavior because without money one has no food, water or shelter. So the control structure buys up the land or controls the land then controls the water supplies then controls the food supplies then everyone has to jump through hoops to get money to get some of that land, food and water so the slave aspect is achieved. This is all a symptom of human beings who have had their minds altered as children by the education and are making unreasonable decisions. The beings that do not get a good education essentially end up with jobs they are not pleased with but because they got enough education to hinder their minds they perceive that the fact they have a "poor" job is because they were not intelligent enough in school. They were not intelligent enough or had bad genes so they deserve the slave job they have so they do not resist that because they just assume the education is the end all be all relative to a beings intelligence. So civilization all across the board is nothing but insane control freaks that own all the water, all the land, all the food sources and if one does not jump through their insane hoops one starves or dies or is deemed a revolutionary and demonized. One indication that the entire control system is insane is because if a person really is in straits they will just go break the law and go to jail and they can get food and water there. This shows that civil disobedience is the weakness of civilization. If every single person on the planet went on welfare then the entire control structure would collapse and that is an indication that the control structure itself is flawed. This is why civilization looks at people on welfare as evil or bad and one is frowned on if they have to go to a homeless shelter. A transient is simply a person who no longer wishes to associate with the control structure and they live in the wild , out in the streets and get their food from the garbage and their water from any source they can.

Once the control structure controls the food and water it is calling the shots. The complexity is the entire system is insane because of the education. Left brain likes to control things and that is contrary to right brain or a being with right brain unveiled so it is logical civilization would want to control the water supply and control the food and control the land and control the people and control everything. As a parent you have no control over what education your child gets because if you attempt to educate your child not using written education, reading and math you will factually go to jail, and thus you as a parent do not even have control over you own child relative to how their mind ends up and thus you are nothing but a minion of the control structure. If you are a child or have no children, your parents are minions of the control structure and your mental state is proof. It appears like a conspiracy but that is not logical.

X = All the powers that be in civilization: governments and rulers of various sorts.
Y = Beings that applied the remedy fully and beings that never got written education.
Z = controlling nature; coveting
A = freedom ; non controlling nature
B = resources

$$X + B = Z$$

$$Y + B = A$$

This means the powers that be in civilization could not possibly be beings that are of sound mind (Y) because sound minded beings are not prone to control things like food, water and shelter and people.

[Exodus 4:21 And the LORD said unto Moses, When thou goest to return into Egypt, see that thou do all those wonders before Pharaoh, which I have put in thine hand: but I will harden his heart, that he shall not let the people go.]

This comment is saying, the control structure will never let the people be free because the control structure is left brain extreme because it got the education and a left brain trait is to control or coveting so it is not the control structure is in some sort of plot to control everything it is simply, the very nature of a being that has right brain veiled by the education has a controlling nature. The opposite of control is loss of control.

Control: to limit or restrict somebody or something.

A law is a form of control. A rule is a form of control.

A rule is if you do not get a good education you cannot get a "good" job.

A law is the compulsory attendance law; all children must be educated starting at age six or seven with reading, writing and math, left brain favoring conditioning aspects.

If you get a good education you get money for food and water and shelter and if you do not like that it is too bad because it is the law, so even if your mind does not take well to the education, you still end up with a nice slave job as a consolation prize.

Consolation: a source of comfort to somebody who is upset or disappointed.

So in order for this to work there has to be a valid appearing explanation for all the people that didn't do so well in school and that explanation is "Your genes were not that good". "You didn't do well at the education because God didn't bless you with intelligence." This argument is believable because by the time one discovers they didn't do so well at the education their right brain traits are already veiled. A child cannot drop out of school before they are sixteen but the education veils right brain by the time the child is ten or even nine. By the age of sixteen the mind is ruined by the education. One reality is the control structure will make all these drugs illegal for the sole purpose of protecting the children's mind and the common peoples mind but the education is infinitely worse for the mind because it is just like a hallucinogenic drug but it never wears off unless one applies the remedy so it is far worse than all drugs combined because drugs wears off eventually and the left brain conditioning for the vast majority never wears off. The deeper reality is when one is of sound mind drugs do not really do much at all relative to altering perception so this means the drugs in fact make a person in that extreme left brain state feel reality a little bit while the drug lasts. So this demonstrates the control structure that is civilization is so mentally ruined by the education it is just doing things only a completely insane aspect would do. There is no rhyme or reason to any of the rules and laws the control structure suggests. It is all just insanity upon insanity. There is no logic at all to mentally hindering people via education, and then locking them in jail for attempting to get relief from that mental hindering, doing drugs. There is no sanity in mentally hindering people, education, and then spending all these resources attempting to find pills to treat all the mental symptoms caused by that education conditioning in the first place. There is no sound logic in putting a child in a mental position they have great depression and then when that child seeks drugs to escape that mental suffering, punish that child for doing that, so it can only be a symptom of insanity. The ancient texts suggest it is a devil or a being is possessed by the darkness but of course insanity is one in the same. If you have an insane person directing traffic you will suffer for it and it is that simple and that insane person is the powers that be in civilization and that includes you and it doesn't include me, I left the cult accidentally. The absolute reality of all of this is after a person gets all that education they are screwed mentally for life unless some sort of miracle happens and that person applies the remedy the full measure, this of course is not including beings in some places that get the oral education until their mind is much more mature because their parents are sane and do not mentally destroy their offspring knowingly or unknowingly. I spoke at length with a being and told her the remedy and I told her about the education and she followed exactly what I was saying and then she said "I will think about the remedy." and I knew she was doomed because she is not able to reason. Other words I am saying "Go mindfully kill yourself to the full measure" and no being with an unsound mind would ever come to the conclusion: "Sure thing, right away." This means the education induced schizophrenia is perhaps permanent for most so it is the most damaging thing in the history of mankind because I am certain I am far past the point of having to prove the education does in fact hinder the mind but even at that it means little because whomever gets it is essentially mentally ruined for life anyway. There is no other way to apply the remedy the full measure but with this mental self control fear not remedy applied one way or another unless one gets into some sort of traumatic accident but in the traumatic accident their brain is harmed so their mind is harmed also. If there are so many people applying this remedy and waking up as some have suggested then the collective understanding in the species would be full of information about the damaging effects of the written educating and math on the mind but the absolute truth is, the ancient texts are the only books on the market that cover the topic in depth but because of when they were written the ones in the education induced schizophrenia can't understand them. We are only talking about mentally killing all the offspring in a permanent fashion, I find it hard to grasp that a sane person would discuss anything else ever. Who cares about the economy, politics, medicine, science, space, government when the offspring are being systematically mentally killed on an industrial scale. It is a simple fact I am surrounded by mentally destroyed human beings that are so mentally destroyed they are factually in another perception dimension completely. They care about money when children are being annihilated and they support it and brag about it and they perceive they are doing a good thing by annihilating all the children mentally and permanently. The only thing I have done that shows wisdom since the accident is I write in diary format. I am perhaps flawless in my explanations but that will never make up for the fact the vast majority that got the education as children are ruined through and through and will never wake up and that means the vast majority will continue to do the same thing to the next generation of children. The scribes celebrate the birth of the truth in the season of death, winter, with Christmas, and the death of the truth in the season of life, spring, with Easter. The scribes celebrate the birth of the truth, the festival of lights, in the season of death, winter, with Hanukkah, and the death of the truth with a story of death in the season of life, spring, with Passover. Peace achieved using control aspects is tyranny. There is no need to be violent if you have a convincing argument.

4/3/2010 5:48:46 PM – This is relative to the final chapter in Exodus, chapter 40.

[Exodus 40:1 And the LORD spake unto Moses, saying,]

This comment is saying Moses who had applied the remedy and was under the influence of right brain, the god image in man and made a determination.

[Exodus 40:3 And thou shalt put therein the ark of the testimony, and cover the ark with the vail.]

[ark of the testimony] This is the remedy to the tree of knowledge, the fear not remedy.

[cover the ark with the vail.] This means the remedy will become occult knowledge or a secret, veiled. The logic in this is to keep the remedy a secret and that way the ones who knew the secret would give it to their children and their children would be very wise in contrast to the ones who never applied the remedy and so they would eventually dominate. It would be like ten people who took a mind hindering drug and then one of those people found the remedy and were very wise in contrast to the ones that were still mentally hindered so that one person would appear to be the ruler or would assume the leadership role simply because they were not mentally hindered. Kind of like I accidentally applied the remedy so I am no longer hallucinating out of my mind and thus any being on this planet that has not applied the remedy stands no chance against my wishes because I am simply far to intelligent in contrast to them in their mentally hindered state. So this concept is an indication that Moses was aware there was no way to stop the neurosis caused by education so the next best thing was to make the best of the situation which is to keep the remedy secret and make sure the ones who did apply the remedy took control but that is not how it worked out because the ones in neurosis see wisdom as foolishness. The ones in neurosis had far greater numbers because they pushed the education on every child and so eventually they were a huge majority and might makes right. One is always a slave to the intelligence of the majority. When drowning stop breathing. Another way to look at it is I can walk up to you and say "fear not" and if you did not understand what that meant relative to restoring your mind after you got the education you would have no clue that is the most powerful ritual and occult knowledge in the history of mankind. Just understanding what fear not means is a source of infinite power because once applied one unveils their right brain and returns to sound mind and in that state of mind they are a cerebral god in contrast to the ones that have not applied the remedy. The deeper reality is a conscious sound minded human being appears very wise in contrast to an unconscious mentally unsound human being and what separates the two in this narrow is the concept "fear not". Any human being on this planet can say "fear not" but very few can understand what it really means and very few of those very few can actually apply it the full measure and they are known as the seekers or the meek.

So the question comes up what is the ark of the covenant? Any human being on the planet that applies the remedy the full measure because then they have the ability to explain the remedy to any human being scribe on the planet. So they are this fountain of wisdom because right brain traits are so powerful at full power one can grasp any concept in no time and explain them to ones that have not applied the remedy and thus enlighten them so to speak. So the ark of the covenant is a person that applies the remedy the full measure so they are valuable to the species because they can attempt to assist the species to wake up but the complexity is that person does not see their self of value so they are like a child. So then there are situations where groups of beings protect the "ark" from the "sinister" because the "ark" is capable of waking up everyone and the "sinister" hates that prospect because misery loves company. So an "ark" is a person that wakes up well and in turn can wake up others well and then they to become "arks"; containers of the covenant.

This comment in the Gospel of Thomas explains it well.

[13 - Jesus said, "I am not your teacher. Because you have drunk, you have become intoxicated from the bubbling spring that I have tended.]

This line is saying, I am not your teacher because I am just an "ark" and since you followed what I suggested "denied yourself" which is a form of the remedy you are now an "ark" or a "bubbling spring" and so now you can assist others to wake up.

So Norah was an ark and his son Abraham was an ark and his son Isaac was an ark and also his relative Lot was an ark and Moses was an ark unto himself because he started a new lineage because he woke up on his own. Jonah was an ark unto himself because he woke up alone. There are many other arks , then the new testament came along and Zacharias explained the fear not covenant to his son John the Baptist and John the Baptist explained it to Jesus and Jesus explained it to the disciples so all of these beings became arks of the covenant or [ark of the testimony]. What testimony? The remedy to the tree of knowledge that is required to restore one's mind or right brain traits after the left brain favoring education veils them. So then after the new testament era Mohammed came along and he started a new lineage and he became an ark and he in turn assisted many with the remedy and they became arks but the complexity is one has to apply the remedy the full measure to become a "big ark". So this means one has to go the full measure with the remedy and that means they have to literally be in a situation their mind says "You will factually die if you do not run from this spooky situation" and then that person answers in their mind with "I do not care at all and I fear not absolutely" and that is the full measure. This means if one is not a big ark they simply have to apply the remedy better. That is what the story of Jonah is suggesting, he was aware he was still afraid when asked to go testify so he threw himself into the sea and that means he applied the remedy the full measure then he was a big ark. Buddha was a big ark in the east but there are many arks and there always will be because no matter what once the education veils right brain, right brain is going to seek to come back into harmony in the mind and that is going to happen no matter what but it is not always a person's decision because a person with their right brain traits veiled is in a sort of slumber so they are not fully aware of it.

The equation is very simple:

A = the mind when one is born; left and right brain aspects in perfect harmony
B = Mind after the education, right brain traits veiled and left brain traits dominate
C = Tendency

The C of B = A

The mind cannot exist in the B state so it is always attempting to go back to the A state. This plays out over a person's entire life of course after they get the education and many never return to the A state and at times the B state is permanent but there is always a chance to return to A state because the tendency of the mind is to return to mental harmony. So there are people that return to the A state in many different ways and thus the comment "all paths lead to one path" the path is the middle way, mental harmony, but since this is not fantasy land some do not survive that journey. Simply put once the mind is bent to the left starting at the age of seven or six by the education it is understood nightmare situations are bound to happen and that nightmare situation is what you call civilization. So you may hear stories about the ark being taken or transported to a safe location. That simply means the person that is the ark is protected from the "sinister", the scribes. Just like the fountain of youth the ark is not a box or a location it is a container or vessel and in this case it's a person that has applied the remedy well and in turn is a [bubbling spring that I have tended] and so they are valuable not because of who they are it is because of what they are, a bubbling spring that can wake up others or assist others to apply the remedy to the "curse" of the tree of knowledge. The ark concept works like this: Did you get the education as a child? If so go sit in a spooky place alone at night and when your mind says "Run or a spook is going to kill you" you simply ignore that over active hypothalamus signal and "fear not". Good luck in burning my books.

4/4/2010 6:19:54 AM – Endangering The Welfare Of A Child Law:

"He or she knowingly directs or authorizes a child under a defined age to engage in an occupation involving a substantial risk of danger to his life or health;"

Occupation: an activity on which time is spent.

School is an activity in which time is spent. Written education is essentially all left brain favoring and since the frontal lobe does not mature until one is twenty that engages the child in a substantial risk of danger to his life or health; health being mental health and that is relative to physical health. This means firstly the governments of the world are guilty of this crime, then the state governments, then the local governments, then the schools' their self, then the teachers in those schools, then the parents of that child and then any being that pays money that supports those schools that teach children the "brand" of education known as reading, writing and math to small children. So in America there are 75 million children in school in any given school year. Now in the term [He or she knowingly directs or authorizes] one must consider Socrates Paradoxes.

[No one errs or does wrong willingly or knowingly.] and the paradox of that comment is [Everyone errs or does wrong willingly or knowingly.] Look at it like this: If the above people mentioned had their right brain traits fully restored they would be fully aware the education mentally hinders the children because they would have their right brain pattern detection and intuition active in the conscious state so that means subconsciously they are fully aware. Other words I had no clue whatsoever seventeen months ago written education and math mentally hindered me but now I am fully aware of it and the only thing that changed is my right brain intuition and pattern detection traits were restored so I was aware of it subconsciously and after I applied the remedy I became consciously aware of it so this comment: [He or she knowingly directs or authorizes] applies. I am not really teaching you anything relative to the dangers of written education I am simply reminding you about what you already know and once it clicks one tends to become sad or depressed. Laws are based on absolutes so they do not consider paradox and that is illogical because paradox is complexity so laws are based on simple black and white judgments and that is a symptom of left brain traits, simple minded linear aspects. One way to look at it is I am [knowingly directs or authorizes] because I am aware when I pay taxes that go to school even if I buy an item and taxes are collected on it I am putting a child at [substantial risk of danger to his life or health;]. I am fully aware I am putting children as risk and you do not but the only difference is I have my "subconscious", right brain aspects, restored to a conscious state of mind because I applied the remedy to the tree of knowledge. I am fully aware I am breaking this law: Endangering The Welfare Of A Child Law and you are not fully aware but you are partially aware but just not on a conscious level because you have not applied the remedy to restore right brain traits after education has veiled them, namely intuition.

[J. M. (13) hanged himself after he was allegedly unfairly punished for bad behavior at school .]

[after he was allegedly unfairly punished for bad behavior at school .] This means this child did not follow directions. So this child is in school with beings that have right brain traits veiled, teachers, and so they are controlling aspects and they determine this child did something bad, probably chewed gum or some other control freak stupidity, and then this child said "I have seen enough of the lunatic asylum, I will catch you on the flip side." The only possible way I could know that is exactly what that child determined in spirit is because I have subconscious aspects in my conscious state and if any being on the planet that has right brain veiled reads that they will say "That is not what happened or that is not what it is saying." But in reality if they had right brain, subconscious, aspect unveiled they would say "yes that is exactly what happened." Beings that sense time are not ignorant on an absolute scale they just have some of their senses or "eyes" blinded, intuition and pattern detection, and when those senses are turned back on they see much better, is one way to look at it. We are dysfunctional as a species because of the ways the written education is taught.

Dysfunctional: characterized by an inability to function emotionally or as a social unit.

I am sitting here writing books explaining why the written education and math mentally hinders the children and the vast majority of the species that got the education is assuming I am not telling the truth or am wrong so we are unable to function as a unit in a cohesive manor because anyone that got the education is unable to think clearly because their extreme emotions are hindering their ability to think clearly. It is one thing to have emotions and it is another thing to have so many emotions one cannot even tell when they are harming children on an industrial scale so the question is when do emotions become deadly relative to one's ability to think and thus function, and the answer is when the entire species is mentally hindering children on an industrial scale and they are not even aware of it as a social unit then that is an indication their emotions are turned up way to high because the emotions are affecting their ability to think clearly and thus the emotions are affecting their cognitive ability. The very odd reality is if I turn myself into the authorities and explain I am fully aware my taxes are used to educate and thus mentally and thus physically harm the children they will say "That's okay there is no evidence written education hinders children mentally and thus physically." because if I am guilty, relative to their logic then everyone is guilty. It is not really possible to have morals in this narrow. Delusional meekness is arrogance.

Morals: relating to issues of right and wrong and to how individual people should behave.

Mentally unsound beings do not know right from wrong and thus they know not what they do.

Morals: based on what somebody's conscience suggests is right or wrong, rather than on what rules or the law says should be done.

The definition of conscience is not even a proper definition. Conscience is intuition and that is a right brain trait and the written education veils that.

[Revelation 17:13 These have one mind, and shall give their power and strength unto the beast.]

[These (the scribes, the ones that sense time) have one mind] = [; the pen of the scribes is in vain.] = in learning to scribe(write) ones veils their right brain because written education is all left brain favoring so a person is left with one mind , a left brain influenced mind and right brain traits are veiled.

[, and shall give their power and strength unto the beast] = What has strength and power? Right brain traits the god image in man; complexity, ambiguity, intuition, pattern detection, lightning fast random access processing. Education gives all the children's strength and power to the beast.

4/7/2010 6:12:10 PM –

[Leviticus 1:1 And the LORD called unto Moses, and spake unto him out of the tabernacle of the congregation, saying,]

[Leviticus 1:2 Speak unto the children of Israel, and say unto them, If any man of you bring an offering unto the LORD, ye shall bring your offering of the cattle, even of the herd, and of the flock.]

[Genesis 3:14 And the LORD God said unto the serpent, Because thou hast done this, thou art cursed above all cattle, and above every beast of the field; upon thy belly shalt thou go, and dust shalt thou eat all the days of thy life:]

[bring your offering of the cattle, even of the herd, and of the flock.] = [Because thou hast done this, thou art cursed above all cattle,]

So in the Leviticus 1:2 Moses is explaining how to bring the sacrifices, the ones cursed above cattle, the scribes, the ones that sense time.

[offering of the cattle, even of the herd, and of the flock] = the scribes. Other words the scribes are sheep because they have their right brain intuition veiled so they cannot think for their self so they can only function when people give them directions. The remedy itself is self sacrifice and that is the covenant. If you go to a dark spooky place alone at night and your mind says run like the wind or you will die and you fear not, you sacrifice yourself mindfully.

Tabernacle: a portable tent used as a sanctuary for the Ark of the Covenant by the Israelites during the Exodus.

What is the Ark? A person that can assist or explain the fear not remedy because they have applied said remedy.

What is the covenant? The fear not remedy that is applied after ones get the written education so they do not go through life with their right brain traits veiled.

covenant: a solemn agreement that is binding on all parties

Who are the parties? Mankind; the human race. The human race can keep the written education and math as long as they keep the covenant. If mankind does not keep the convent they will all have their right brain traits veiled and then mankind will destroy the environment and their self and the children and it will become a whoredom, relative to: [Ezekiel 23:17 And the Babylonians(scribes) came to her into the bed of love(emotions), and they defiled her with their whoredom(written education), and she was polluted with them(right brain traits were veiled), and her mind(right brain traits veiled, strong left brain traits= unsound mind) was alienated from them(the kindred, the ones with no sense of time that had sound minds).

Whoredom is relative to idolatry. Idolatry is relative to excessive admiration or love shown for somebody or something relative to control and thus coveting. A false god is relative to written language, it was called demotic which means popular. After one gets the written language they become very material focused because their cerebral aspects are reduced so all they have left is material aspects because their cerebral aspects are hindered.

[excessive admiration or love shown for somebody or something.] = Lust, greed, envy, coveting and this is relative to the psychological aspects one exhibits because their right brain random access is veiled. One cannot covet or be greedy or be lustful if their thought patterns are changing on a second to second basis because their right brain random access aspect is in their conscious mind.

So if one applies this tabernacle aspect to the Abraham and Isaac explanation of the remedy.

[Genesis 22:7 And Isaac spake unto Abraham his father, and said, My father: and he said, Here am I, my son. And he said, Behold the fire and the wood: but where is the lamb for a burnt offering?] [Here am I] is out of sequence it should be [Here I am] = right brain random access factoring into the authors writing or perception.

First Isaac is the sacrifice and he must be sacrifice because he got the education as a child as explained here : [Genesis 21:4 And Abraham circumcised his son Isaac being eight days old, as God had commanded him.]

[circumcised his son Isaac being eight days old]= Got the written education as a young child.

[And he said, Behold the fire and the wood: but where is the lamb for a burnt offering?] This comment is explaining the "sacrifice" cannot know they are going to be sacrificed. Isaac is saying "I see you are going to make a sacrifice but who is the sacrifice?" This is required relative to the version of the remedy because if the person knows then the remedy will not work. Another way to look at it is, if you know for a fact nothing will happen to you if you go to a dark spooky place alone at night then you will never be able to apply the remedy. This is a complexity of the remedy, there has to be a chance something will kill you literally relative to your perception in that dark spooky place. It could just be a 5% chance but that is enough of a chance one does not have absolute certainty. It is a mind exercise and that means the person doing the sacrifice has to believe there is a chance they will die literally and once their mind says "You will die from this spooky place" they fear not. So the concept of the remedy itself means one has to fool their self. [And he(Isaac) said, Behold the fire and the wood: but where is the lamb for a burnt offering?] This is an indication Abraham knew he was not going to kill Isaac but Isaac did not know that. So relative to this explanation of the remedy, the ark is Abraham, the tabernacle is this alter Isaac was on and the sacrifice was Isaac and the covenant was the fear not remedy the ark, Abraham, was applying on Isaac.

So this line relative to the Abraham and Isaac explanation of the remedy is:

[If any man of you bring an offering unto the LORD (Abraham), ye shall bring your offering of the cattle (Isaac), even of the herd, and of the flock.]

44

So this is an indication at the time of Leviticus this applying the remedy aspect had gone underground and the only people that were considered to have this remedy applied were the meek among the scribes and the Lords children. This is relative to the scribes when they suggest "A cult preys on the depressed and suicidal." Or the scribes will say "People who are well educated do not tend to get mixed up in cults or taken advantage of by cults." This is why education has this certain "popular" aspect and is assumed to obviously make one wise. The scribes are saying "If you have a good education you are not prone to be a sucker." But the very fact they got the education and it veiled their right brain proves they are infinite suckers. One cannot be more of a sucker than to take part in a ritual that veils their right brain and turns them from an infinitely wise being to a ten percent cerebral function being essentially permanently. So the concept suggested by the scribes is "People who are well educated do not tend to get caught up in cults" is really a scare tactic or a pride tactic. The only scribes that are capable of applying the remedy intentionally are the meek scribes and meek is depressed and suicidal scribes because that is the state of mind one has to be in to apply the remedy and that state of mind is an indication right brain is starting to unveil.

The freedom of religion aspect is very complex because relative to the remedy the scenario would be, a person goes into this "tent" and all they know is they are going to be sacrifice and killed, and the "priests" or the "lords" know they are not going to kill that person, they are going to make that person mindful of death and then that person is going to "let go" when they perceive death is there. So this again is just a mind exercise but relative to laws of today, that "sacrifice" is going to perceive it is attempted murder. It is similar to the Vincent Prince movies where he pays people ten thousand dollars to stay in the haunted house over night, that concept is attempted murder. If you go to a spooky place alone at night seeking the shadow of death that is attempted suicide. So relative to the New testaments, John the Baptist was attempting murder one the "sacrifices" with his water remedy and Jesus adapted that and turned it into attempted suicide when he said "deny yourself" or 'those who lose their life (mindfully) preserve it." So Jesus turned this situation from an "attempted murder" remedy to an "attempted suicide remedy" and that took away the "liability" aspects, and that means anyone can apply this remedy on an individual level and no one else is required. So that took away the need for "priests" and religious leaders because once a person understood the concept they could go apply it their self. This perhaps caused some trouble because in fact it negated this Torah aspect where you have priests that apply the remedy. So Jesus kind of destroyed the hierarchy and that played out in an obvious way in Islam because in Islam there is no "chief priest", everyone is equal relative to the congregation, so to speak.

[Matthew 27:12 And when he was accused of the chief priests and elders, he answered nothing.]

[he (Jesus)was accused of the chief priests and elders] This is suggesting the Jesus pulled the rug out from the power struggle or the hierarchy because Jesus explained the remedy so any person could apply the remedy by their self and on their own but this is not exactly what it appears. This was not a struggle between the kindred, the ones with no sense of time. This was taking the power away from the false teachers. The ones with no sense of time are outnumbered by the vast armies of the scribes so they are not concerned one way or another because they cannot win anyway so the only beings that were upset about Jesus explaining the remedy so anyone could apply it for their self were the False teachers, the Scribe priests, because they are not even aware of the remedy they are just in it for the money and power and their lust and greed for power and money. Another way to look at it is, whatever you have to do you convince yourself to apply the remedy is allowed because on an absolute scale the scribes are going to put more children into the neurosis with the education that need to apply the remedy on a yearly basis than people will apply the remedy to the full measure. It would be like two people in a foxhole in a war, and they do not like each other or they both think for their self and they are looking on the battle field at the enemy that has them outnumbered a million against two. So although those two may not see eye to eye in that foxhole, the reality is they are not going to get in each other's way because at the end of the day it is just those two against a vast army. You can think for yourself because the right brain intuition once unveiled means you can make your own decisions, one does not wait around for permission so to a speak about the remedy. I only have experience with the full measure remedy and so I have to do a lot more writing because the full measure remedy means it is the hardest version of the remedy to apply. My chances are .0024% to convince any scribe to apply it so I have to write a lot more and do a lot more convincing.

X = full measure remedy where one reaches absolute consciousness, left and right brain in perfect harmony.
Y = lukewarm remedy where one still has a sense of time but they are awake to a degree
Z = has not applied the remedy at all
A = Sammasambuddhas attain buddhahood, then decide to teach others the truth they have discovered= Lords
B= Paccekabuddhas, sometimes called "silent Buddhas" are similar to sammasambuddhas in that they attain nirvana and acquire many of the same powers as a sammasambuddha, but are unable to teach what they have discovered. = Disciples or minor Lords
C = Scribe; one that got the written education or associated with scribes too much; contact

C + X = A
C + Y = B
C + Z = C

If you apply the remedy to a degree but you are [unable to teach what they have discovered.] then you need to apply the remedy better or apply the full measure remedy. This is what the story of Jonah was explaining. Jonah applied the remedy lukewarm and was still showing signs of a fear, so he was only at the level of Paccekabuddhas:

[Jonah 1:2 Arise, go to Nineveh, that great city, and cry against it; for their wickedness is come up before me.

Jonah 1:3 (But Jonah rose up to flee)=(still had fear) unto Tarshish from the presence of the LORD...]

So then Jonah applied the full measure remedy, fully letting go [Jonah 1:12 And he said unto them, Take me up, and (cast me forth into the sea);] and then he reached Sammasambuddhas which is heaven or the ideal plane or consciousness and then he started by teaching the King of the city [the truth they (he) have discovered]

[Jonah 3:2 Arise, go unto Nineveh, that great city, and preach unto it the preaching that I bid thee.

[Jonah 3:3 So Jonah arose, and went unto Nineveh, according to the word of the LORD.] = No fear]

[Jonah 3:6 For word came unto the king of Nineveh, and he arose from his throne, and he laid his robe from him, and covered him with sackcloth, and sat in ashes.] = Jonah humbled that King of that city because he reached absolute consciousness and could explain his case flawlessly. Of course this is not fantasy land. Even if every country in the world decided to make every person apply the remedy that vast majority could not because it is quite a mental exercise to apply the remedy to full measure relative to the person's state of mind after the education. That is an indication the written education taught to a child and the resulting neurosis is essentially in most cases permanent.

[Sammasambuddhas attain buddhahood, then decide to teach others the truth they have discovered.] So to even be a Sammasambuddhas one has to first get the written education, then apply the remedy the full measure. So the human beings that are above a Sammasambuddhas are the tribes which are human beings that have no contact with "civilization" and never got the reading , writing and math education, they are and have always been fully conscious. Although the scribes will suggest the "tribes" are foolish, at least the tribes do not destroy their own offspring mentally with the "wisdom" education nor do they pass laws that make it against the law not to destroy the offspring's minds with the "wisdom" education and the tribes also do not brag about how they destroy their own offspring mentally starting at the age of seven with the "wisdom" education and not even know it. So the Sammasambuddhas wish they were of the tribes and this is why in some cases beings that wake up leave civilization all together and go live in the wilderness, simply because they cannot take the suffering they are aware of when they are in the cities so machine state is what one seeks and that is why the full measure remedy is the way to go. Of course Socrates suggested "Where can I run?" and that pretty much sums it up. The scribes are everywhere it is very hard to run from them and thus run from their suffering. There is a being known as the Buddha boy in India and he essentially spends long periods in the wilderness alone and once in a while comes back to civilization and recently when he returned he said something along the lines of "There is so much suffering" and then he grabs his sword and heads back out into the wilderness. The deeper reality is once one applies the remedy and gets warmed up a bit they are in a totally different perception dimension, the no sense of time perception dimension so they can block most of the suffering aspects they are aware of as a result of the strong right brain intuition but it takes some time to get good at it. Perhaps it is more along the line of what Malcolm X said "Anger is a gift". The suffering is a gift so instead of running from it look at it as a way to better yourself because if you see it as a demon you are going to perhaps have issues.

[Leviticus 1:10 And if his offering be of the flocks, namely, of the sheep, or of the goats, for a burnt sacrifice; he shall bring it a male without blemish.]

[he shall bring it a male without blemish.] Notice this is speaking about the males. Why would they be talking about males? Because the females were not likely to get the written education in this time period. This means females at this time could not read, write or do math. Any one of those three aspects would cause the left brain favoring neurosis. The males were the ones taught those inventions. This chapter of Leviticus is very heavy on details. It is giving all these aspects about a ritual to sacrifice animals [sheep, or of the goats]. Male sheep or goats. These are just key words for male scribes, males that sense time, males that have the curse caused by the tree of knowledge. So this elaborate "sacrifice" situation is set up to give off the impression to the "sheep and goats" that they will in fact be literally sacrificed but in reality they are only mindfully sacrificed. As long as one focuses on these two comment in the text:

Reason one has to apply the remedy the covenant:[Genesis 2:17 But of the tree of the knowledge of good and evil, thou shalt not eat of it: for in the day that thou eatest thereof thou shalt surely die.]

The remedy or covenant: [Genesis 15:1 After these things the word of the LORD came unto Abram in a vision, saying, Fear not, Abram: I am thy shield, and thy exceeding great reward.]

It is an "if then" statement:

If one gets [tree of the knowledge of good and evil](written language and math) then [Fear not remedy must be applied].

What this indicates is, firstly it is difficult enough to apply the fear not remedy and considering the entire species keeps pushing the tree of knowledge on the offspring with reckless abandon this comment cannot possibly be literally talking about sacrificing actual sheep and goats, because that would serve no purpose.

[Leviticus 1:10 And if his offering be of the flocks, namely, of the sheep, or of the goats, for a burnt sacrifice; he shall bring it a male without blemish.]

It is the same as circumcising. Literal circumcision of a child at eight days has no possible effects on the child relative to assisting that child to apply the fear not remedy after they get the tree of knowledge much later in life, starting at the age of seven or six.

The main argument is: [Genesis 1:10 And God called the dry land Earth; and the gathering together of the waters called he Seas: and God saw that it was good.]

The being see's holistically, without prejudice, when right hemisphere is at 50% so a person's perception is holistic, a right brain trait. Other words they do not have prejudice so to assume God would see Earth and the Sea as good relative to [and God saw that it was good.] and then God says but I want you to physically harm the male children with literal circumcising, is factually not probable. God see's everything in the subset of earth and the Sea as good but then a male child in that subset he wants to be harmed or cut suggests God does have prejudice, and that is not logical. God is either prejudice or not and this (Gen 1:10) comment suggest God is not prejudice and that is in line with a right brain holistic aspects and this holistic aspect is what one has in a sound mind state. Simply put God does not create things and then finds fault or becomes prejudice with them because that would suggest he makes mistakes. This suggests God does not make mistakes: [And God

49

called the dry land Earth; and the gathering together of the waters called he Seas: and God saw that it was good.] So this means the whole concept of circumcision is relative to an adjustment or adaptation relative to the tree of knowledge. It is like saying "Yes teach the children written education and math so "sacrifice them early" but then be prepared to assist them with the covenant, the fear not remedy."

What is all comes down to relative to these texts is, they are written in code and that means a human being has to have intuition, pattern detection, complexity, random access processing and ambiguity at full power to ever be able to understand these texts and if one has those right brain traits missing they will take these texts as all simple literals and these texts will harm them. That is an absolute. As human beings we are actually cutting the males penis, because some mental abomination that never applied the fear not remedy assumed they know what these texts mean. If you perceive God wants us to cut the small tiny innocent males penis when they are 8 days old you are either the devil himself or much worse than the devil himself. God is not prejudice and that means God would not find fault with what he creates but the sinister would find fault with what God creates. Perhaps you should ponder that carefully. These are holy texts and if any being that is not holy, does not have right brain the god image of man unveiled attempts to use these texts they will never do anything but harm their self and that is what these texts want them to do. These texts have a built in complexity that if any being with right brain veiled attempts to apply these texts they will harm their self, destroy their temple, and perhaps harm others in the process and perhaps even apply the remedy in the process of "destroying their temple". Another way to look at it is a person that applies the remedy the full measure is in the machine state so it is logical the full impact of these texts even as they write is beyond their understanding because they are in the now. If one thinks about a war situation let's say world war two. The allies planted some papers on a dead man and dumped him off the coast of France with the understanding the Axis would find the body and find the plans and react to the information in those plans. These ancient texts were written so if they were ever found by the scribes they would inflict maximum damage on the scribes who attempted to teach them. Consider this, The Torah the New Testament and the Quran are all saying the extract same thing in spirit but the scribes have turned them into 3 separate religions and beliefs and they have been killing each other over that division for hundreds of years. Simply put I do not detect any Muslim country any Jewish country or any Christian country speaking out against the dangers of written education on the minds of the children so I do not detect any of them got these texts right. They are all scribes and all missed the point. Why don't you determine which country speaks out against the dangers of written education and math and which country also suggests the fear not remedy or a version of it after a child gets the written education and math and you will understand no one has a clue.

Hope: a feeling that something desirable is likely to happen.

I do not have a feeling any country in this narrow is even close to pondering if written education and math perhaps have some unwanted mental side effects on the children considering the child's mind does not even develop, the frontal lobe, until the child is twenty. I do not know what hope is and I ponder if your hope is not simply another one of your delusions. I am attempting to communicate with human beings that have been mentally aborted and thus have zero cognitive ability. I say potato and they hear tomato and that never changes into infinity. I cannot write fast enough to make up for the fact I am speaking to human beings with zero cognitive ability. I tell them to put some water on their self because they are on fire and they instead jump into a pool of gasoline. I suggest the written education and math are very left brain favoring and factually does harm the minds of seven year old children and I was one of them they say "That is not possible at all no matter what ever." They have lost their cognitive ability completely. They are no longer able to reason at all so they are factually insane. The scribes are allowed to make decisions relative to the safety and well being of children and then you suggest you have hope and you have love and you are of God.

[Jeremiah 8:8 How do ye say, We are wise, and the law of the LORD is with us? Lo, certainly in vain made he it; the pen of the scribes is in vain.]

I want you to write a book and explain to the universe how you have the image of God in you when in learning to write and math you veiled the image of God in you, right brain traits. [How do ye say, We are wise, and the law of the LORD is with us?] How do you say you are of God when you are not of God? How do you deceive yourself so easily? Perhaps you have been deceiving yourself for so long you see your lies as truth and your deceit as wisdom.

Vanity: excessive pride, especially in personal appearance. = [Matthew 7:15 Beware of false prophets, which come to you in sheep's clothing, but inwardly they are ravening wolves.] = [Luke 20:46 Beware of the scribes, which desire to walk in long robes, and love greetings in the markets, and the highest seats in the synagogues, and the chief rooms at feasts;]

[come to you in sheep's clothing] = [which desire to walk in long robes] = [excessive pride, especially in personal appearance]

[Beware of false prophets] = [Beware of the scribes]

My paradox is infinite and that statement is also a paradox.

Paradox: a statement, proposition, or situation that seems to be absurd or contradictory, but in fact is or may be true.

The reverse of a paradox is: a statement, proposition, or situation that seems to be sane or logical, but in fact is or may be false.

It is assumed by the scribes the more education one gets the wiser they are and that is assumed to be sane and logical but it is totally false.

4/8/2010 3:45:11 PM - I have to stop assuming you are educating the children because you are not.

Educating: to give knowledge to or develop the abilities of somebody by teaching

You are not developing the abilities of the children with the reading, writing and math you are factually hindering their abilities. You are hindering their right brain creativity, intuition, complexity, pattern detection so that is not developing abilities that is hindering abilities. So educating the children is a bad thing. You can accomplish this [to give knowledge] orally to the children and that will not hinder them. Save all the reading writing and math until the child has developed. What is your rush?

Death: the destruction or extinction of something.

The hindering of the mind by the education means the right brain traits are veiled and thus the destruction of the mind is accomplished so the mind dies, it can be resurrected and born again but that is no easy feat in this narrow.

Death: the destruction or extinction of something.

Extinction is a symptom of an end and an end is a time based concept. In infinity extinction is not possible because there is no beginning and thus no end. I am unable to ever repeat myself because I am in infinity.

Repeat: produce, or experience something again or several times.

[again or several times] The spirit of these word arrangements suggest time. "Again" is time based and "several times" is time based. I am not repeating anything I say, I simply am saying the same thing in many different ways into infinity. Mohammed spoke of these mouths and voices that are all speaking different languages and they calculated the amount of voices were in the trillion range.

"70,000 heads, each head having 70,000 mouths, each mouth having 70,000 tongues, each tongue speaking 70,000 languages; and every one involved in singing God's (Allah's) praises." After calculation this would mean the angel spoke 31,000 trillion languages for the praise of Allah."- Wikipedia.com

The above comment is suggesting the voice of oneness. The spirit of oneness, The holistic voice. Once you apply the remedy you will find and hear and see it everywhere and you will hear it from beings that have not applied the remedy and hear it in music and hear it in nature and hear it in words and sounds and you will eventually only hear that one voice and you will slowly understand there is only that one voice.

[Genesis 1:10 And God called the dry land Earth; and the gathering together of the waters called he Seas: and God saw that it was good.]

This line is suggesting God is observing his creation but not exactly involved in it. Everything is created of God but that does not mean God is in this universe because he is an outside observer and it is illogical God would seek to "fix" his creation since he sees no fault with it to begin with [and God saw that it was good.] God has no prejudice so it is not logical God is attempting to "fix" anything so then we have our species and we are required to remedy this situation we have created relative to what education has done to us. God is simply not going to "fix" what he does not see needs fixing.

[God saw that it was good.] This is not saying "God saw the need to fix things" So we are left to our own devices and perhaps God knows we can get ourselves out of this situation the education has put us in and perhaps that is the test. Perhaps it would be boring if we didn't have situations to ponder and come to further understanding from, one might suggest. There is not much else to do in infinity but come to further understandings. All understandings are of equal value in infinity.

God is dry land and the sea and everything in it so God is everything and this voice in turn is everything and everywhere and is in music and writings and words and sounds and pictures and it everywhere and nothing else is happening at all but this one voice. So it is not logical the written education and math can be bad on their own merits but they are simply tools and if used in a certain fashion, as in taught to children long before their minds develop, they can alter the child's mind and thus perception so that child can no longer hear the voices of oneness that is everywhere. You were one of those children and you can no longer hear the voice that is everywhere. One might suggest I hear wisdom coming out of the mouth of fools. When one has no prejudice one has no prejudice so it is impossible to hold a grudge or be angry because everyone is walking around and saying things I find no fault with but they have been separated from the voice of oneness, right brain holistic aspects, so they are not aware of what is going on around them. The scribe's wires have been crossed so to speak as a result of all that left brain favoring education. I have to use self control to achieve prejudice and the scribes have to use self control to avoid prejudice. The scribes hear one voice or sound and assume it is a bad voice or sound and hear another voice and assume it is a good voice so they have a partial aversion to the voice of oneness that is everywhere and that is abnormal and thus they are cut off from the voice of oneness that is everywhere. This is what the scribes know as prejudice and that is what you may know as left brain seeing parts.

So now we have established educating really means mentally hindering the development of the children. Attempt to look at education as a drug. Here is the scenario:

There are two adults and they want to take a drug that alters their perception. They are very hardcore drug users and they have tried all the known drugs but none of them really did it for them so they kept experimenting and they found a drug more powerful than all other drugs. The drug was called reading, writing and math and although it took a few years of administering this drug, the perception altering aspect was essentially permanent. So one can contrast say LSD or Peyote and one can understand those drugs do alter perception but relative to a clock only for about twelve hours. Then contrast that with what the reading, writing and math do relative to altering perception, which is a lifelong perception altering. So all that left brain favoring education bends the mind to the left and totally alters ones perception from a holistic perception to a seeing parts or prejudice perception and a side effect is one becomes very afraid and thus paranoid. An example of the paranoid aspect is, just by suggesting you go to the spookiest cemetery or abandoned house in the woods alone at night the very first thing that enters your mind is "maybe something will kill me or harm me there" and that is because you are paranoid. Your hypothalamus is telling you there is a possibility that a ghost, goblin or crazy person might kill you in that spooky place and that is paranoia that is a result of your altered perception caused by the education, which is really a mind altering and perception altering drug. It is not education if you are paranoid and hallucinating when you are done with the education, only a drug alters your perception and changes your state of consciousness.

Dimension: a level of consciousness, existence, or reality.

Consciousness: the state of being awake and aware of what is going on around you.

So, you got this perception altering drug called written education and math and it changed your level of consciousness which means you went to another perception dimension and instead of being awake and aware of what is going on around you it made you unconscious and not aware of what is going on around you. You are not aware education is a perception altering drug. I am aware of that so I am awake and aware of what is going on around me and you are asleep and not aware of what is going on around you. I accidentally negated the mental side effects of the perception altering drug and you have not. So in that respect I am not so much telling you what to do as I am telling you I negated the perception altering effects of the drug we both took that you call education. It is logical you would not believe that because your level of consciousness is altered so you are not awake and thus not aware of what is going on around you. So we have these two adults who found this powerful mind altering, perception altering, level of conscious altering drug they called written education or demotic and it was popular because demotic means popular. So it is just like two adults that are on drugs and they say "Give some to the child it will be fun." And so you were that child the adult's gave the drug to you, and now you are high on the drug and because the drug essentially permanently alters your level of consciousness, puts you in another dimension of consciousness, you are not aware of what is going on around you. So I am saying this fear not remedy will negate the effects of the level of consciousness altering drug because I got that level of consciousness altering drug and I negated those effects with the fear not remedy or antidote. You can call the antidote anything you are pleased to call it as long as at the end of the day you take the antidote. Simply put you are harming people in your altered level of consciousness and I am going to stop you by convincing you to take the antidote or I am going to expose you thoroughly as a crazy person that should be locked up and ignored and looked at as a mental abomination that is less than a human being. I am going to expose you as an outcast in the species that harms innocent children. You are in a situation where I am offering you an opportunity to take the antidote but if you mock that and ignore that it may have consequences relative to your safety you may not be pleased with. I am not suggesting you took the level of consciousness altering drug by your own merits I am suggesting the adults gave you the level of consciousness drug so it is not your fault but if you do not take the antidote after it is offered to you that is your fault and the consequences for not taking the antidote may have a direct impact on your safety. I am suggesting the species is weaning itself off this level of consciousness altering drug we started taking 5400 years ago and if you are unwilling to apply the antidote you are no longer going to be considered as a part of the species but instead a threat to the safety of the species and a threat to the offspring of the species and the species has zero tolerance when it comes to the safety of the offspring. You are not more important than the offspring and if you do not apply the antidote you are a threat to the offspring so you are a threat to the species and the species does not tolerate threats to the species. It is wise if you just go and apply the antidote or the remedy because this process that has started is not reversible and that means you are either going to wake up and come back into the fold of the species or you are going to be considered an outcast and threat to the species and treated as such. You are not more important than what you call the species and you are not more important than the offspring. - 5:22:09 PM

4/9/2010 1:45:11 AM –

A comment by Hakuin Ekaku (1686–1769 or 1685–1768) was one of the most influential figures in Japanese Zen Buddhism.

"A beautiful Japanese girl whose parents owned a food store lived near Hakuin. One day, without any warning, her parents discovered she was with child. This made her parents angry. She would not confess who the man was, but after much harassment at last named Hakuin. In great anger the parent went to the master. "Is that so?" was all he would say. After the child was born it was brought to Hakuin. By this time he had lost his reputation, which did not trouble him, but he took very good care of the child. He obtained milk from his neighbors and everything else the child needed. A year later the girl could stand it no longer. She told her parents the truth - the real father of the child was a young man who worked in the fish market. The mother and father of the girl at once went to Hakuin to ask forgiveness, to apologize at length, and to get the child back. Hakuin was willing. In yielding the child, all he said was: "Is that so?""

(from Reps, Paul; Nyogen Senzaki. Zen Flesh, Zen Bones: A Collection of Zen and Pre-Zen Writings. ISBN 0-8048-3186-6.)

The spirit of this text is firstly ambiguity a right brain trait and secondly submission which is relative to lack to pride or ego. If a woman came to you and said "You are the father of my child" and you understood you were not, you perhaps would fight it and suggest you are not and perhaps see it as a struggle or something unwanted. Not questioning what is before you has a lot to do with ambiguity, a right brain trait. The depth of the water is less important than the depth one is willing to go. The water is only cold if you perceive it is cold. There are only demons if you perceive there are demons. What happens to you is less important than how you react to what happens to you. How one reacts under pressure is not always what one thinks under pressure so getting the two in alignment is of value. Notice this is a question "Is that so?" and that is what ambiguity is. If you question everything you doubt everything and that is favoring right brain. Small children ask "Why?" a lot and that is because their right brain ambiguity is not veiled yet by the education. The only way to progress swiftly in intelligence is to doubt everything. I welcome you to doubt the remedy and that may lead you to questioning the remedy and that may led you to attempting the remedy in a spirit of doubt. The moment you stop doubting, you start settling, and that hinders potential intelligence. Sometimes what appears proper is improper so ambiguity is paramount. What you do not question is always your weakness.

[By this time he had lost his reputation, which did not trouble him, but he took very good care of the child.] The spirit of this comment is along the lines of adaptation and showing no fear in a situation or in a time of trouble.

[he had lost his reputation, which did not trouble him] This is showing no ego or pride and indifference to humiliation. One might suggest when Job lost everything he had, that included his reputation.

[Jonah 1:12 And he said unto them, Take me up, and cast me forth into the sea;] = [he had lost his reputation, which did not trouble him] = The meek shall inherit the earth.= submission.

One's ability to submit is relative to ones pride and ego.

Grace: a capacity to tolerate, accommodate, or forgive people.

Accommodate: to be adaptable enough to allow something without major change.

To be adaptable. So people showed up and blamed Hakuin [great anger the parent went to the master. "Is that so?" was all he would say.] The people in the boat blamed Jonah for causing the storm in the sea and Jonah said [Jonah 1:12 And he said unto them, Take me up, and cast me forth into the sea;] This of course is relative to being open minded. Being open minded when one has to sacrifice their self is relative to being adaptable to any situation. Adapting to a situation where you end up building yourself up is called arrogance. Adapting to a situation that causes you "harm" gracefully is relative to humility. These are concepts and things to ponder more than ways of life. For example a person with lots of ego and pride would have perhaps never said "Take me up, and cast me forth into the sea;' so that comment is showing humility. Think about a situation where a person claims another person is the father of a child and that person fights that and says "Prove that is my child or I will not take care of that child." Situations are not always what they appear on face value and that is why adaptation is so important and that is relative to right brain pattern detection, intuition and ambiguity. Adaptation is more along the lines of going with the flow instead of always fighting the flow and resisting the flow. Misfortune arrives and instead of looking at that as punishment one looks at that as a challenge or as daily bread so they can ponder it and come to further understandings instead of attempting to judge that situation and label that situation as proper or improper. Once a person determines a situation is improper they will resist it but grace is relative to accommodation. This of course opens one up to be taken advantage of.

The spirit of this section is being taken advantage of or submission:

"In great anger the parent went to the master. "Is that so?" was all he would say. After the child was born it was brought to Hakuin. By this time he had lost his reputation, which did not trouble him, but he took very good care of the child. He obtained milk from his neighbors and everything else the child needed. A year later the girl could stand it no longer. She told her parents the truth - the real father of the child was a young man who worked in the fish market. The mother and father of the girl at once went to Hakuin to ask forgiveness, to apologize at length, and to get the child back. Hakuin was willing. In (yielding) the child, all he said was: "Is that so?"

[yielding] : inclined to give or bend under pressure = adapt

Rights are trusting. They can be taken advantage of by "lefts" just a like a child can have "candy" easily stolen from them, so to speak.

A sounded minded person is a right because right brain traits rule when the mind is in harmony because right brain has by far stronger traits: Intuition, pattern detection, complexity. The deeper reality is anyone that got the education has to apply the full measure remedy to return to full sound mental harmony.

This "taking candy from a baby" comment is explaining exactly what happened to the Africans, the Incas, the Native Americans and many other "Tribes" down through history that never had the written education or math. So the beings with right brain at 50% are of sound mind, are tribes, but they have very little ego or pride so they have no prejudice so in turn a "left", scribes, will take advantage of them and they may not even mention it because the "rights" do not really see being taken advantage of as an improper thing but just a thing, no judgment or labels, no improper or proper but just a situation that is before them. This is the core problem of what this written education has done to the species. It has thrown the species into this "left brain willing to take advantage of others" divide. The lefts, the ones seeking to control, and the rights, the ones indifferent to control. This means the ones that sense time, the lefts, have to apply self control to not be so controlling and the rights have to apply self control to achieve a mindset of control. What that means is our species is divided or has a rift.

Rift: a gap or break in something where it has split apart.

The rift for the last 5400 years is the scribes versus the tribes. The lefts versus the sound minded. There is no such thing as a left brain leaning person of sound mind because in sound mind right brain traits dominate. This means there are no beings that sense time that are sound minded because in a sound mind when right brain is at 50% the paradox aspect of right brain figures into ones perception and they no longer are able to mindfully sense time. The reason a person mindfully senses time is because the education has veiled their right brain aspects because the written education favors left brain starting at the age of seven long before the mind even develops which is at the age of twenty and is relative to the frontal lobe and that is relative to cognitive ability. So when one thinks back on our history and see's how we took advantage the Native Americans, and took advantage of the Africans and many other tribes one is actually looking at the fruits and deeds of mentally insane beings. Simply put mentally insane people take advantage of their own species for material gains and that means mentally insane people harm their own species for an inanimate object and that is insanity or relative to the lack of cognitive ability. If one goes around taking advantage of their own species they in fact harm their self because they are of that species and that is insanity or self harming and is a symptom of lack of cognitive ability or what is known as common sense. If one goes around shooting their self in the foot they are eventually going to end up on the ground. Economics is based on competition with other beings in the species and that is insanity and self defeating and a symptom the cognitive abilities are not sound. Reality is not about "Me, me , me" it is about "Us, us, us". You charge someone usury rates and you make money from that but you harm that being you charge usury rates to and so you harm the species and thus harm yourself. It is all elementary common sense but insane people know nothing of common sense.

To quote one wise being:

Muhammed asked his male followers to "Be good to women; for they are powerless captives (awan) in your households. You took them in God's trust, and legitimated your sexual relations with the Word of God, so come to your senses people, and hear my words ...".- Wikipedia.com

[come to your senses people] = You must apply the remedy so you can restore your right brain traits like intuition and pattern detection which are senses and once they are restored you will achieve what is known in reality world where I live as cognitive ability. Simply put without your right brain senses like intuition and pattern detection at full power in your conscious state you are factually unable to ever make common sense decisions because intuition factually plays a role in cognitive ability so if that aspect is veiled or hindered even one degree cognitive ability is abnormal.

Cognition: the mental faculty or process of acquiring knowledge by the use of reasoning, intuition, or perception.

After the education your intuition is veiled because the education favors left brain and thus veils right brain aspects and that means your perception is altered so since your perception and intuition is hindered your cognitive ability is hindered.[the use of reasoning, intuition, or perception.] If you don't have the intuition you don't have the proper perception and thus you don't have reasoning abilities. Every year you vote to veil the children's right brain starting at the age of six or seven so you cannot be any more factually stupid.

Stupid: regarded as showing a lack of intelligence, perception, or common sense.

When you mentally destroy the offspring and you are not even aware of it because your intuition is gone because as a child you were mentally destroyed you enter the level of an unviable being that is a threat to their self and to those around them and then you enter the level of an outcast in your own species and you must be dealt with using extreme prejudice because you are nothing but a rabid animal. I ponder what your vote or your opinion means now. Perhaps you should call your cult leader and ask them to think for you because I just explained why you cannot think at all. Silly pattern detection. I am pleased to understand I was very delusional when I thought you would be a contest.

Pathetic: provoking or expressing feelings of compassion and pity.

Pity : a sad or regrettable thing. = [Genesis 6:6 And it repented the LORD that he had made man(the scribes) on the earth, and it grieved him at his heart.]

Repented: to feel regret about a sin or past actions and change your ways or habits.

Maybe we should experiment with not killing all the children mentally starting at the age of six just for chuckles. Perhaps that is unreasonable relative to your perception I pity the blind that once could see. - 4:43:14 PM

The Native Americans easily had their land and resources and freedom stolen from them. The tribes in the Amazon today are easily having their land and resources stolen from them.

[Exodus 2:19 And they said, An Egyptian(Moses, who applied the remedy and left civilization) delivered us(protected us) out of the hand of the shepherds(the left brain control freaks), and also drew water enough for us(took back our natural resources), and watered the flock.]

So a "right" is not concerned with ego and pride, they are concerned with patterns and adapting. So I am aware of this reality [Rights are trusting] so I am mindful to adapt to it. One way to look at it is I am explaining the remedy to the written education neurosis and if a left wishes to patent that and control the explanation of the remedy I will not be concerned with that because that will serve my purpose to spread the explanation of the remedy. So although it may appear like I am being taken advantage of in reality my purpose is to spread the explanation of the remedy and so anything that does that I am willing to accept and be open minded to. So the illusion is I can be taken advantage of and so a left that takes advantage of me from their perspective is in fact being taken advantage of as long as my explanation of the remedy is furthered. Something along the lines of, I am willing to lose all the battles if it leads me to winning the war. The ability to take many loses shows one can roll with the punches or adapt. A loss leads one to further understandings as equally as a win. Once one determines what they are going to do and what one is not going to do, one isolates their self and limits their options and so one becomes their own enemy. I am dealing with beings that were robbed of their cognitive ability so morals, ego and pride do not mean anything. You desire to make people accept you or be pleased with you is based on ego. The deeper reality is the left brain control structure pushed this left brain education on me as a child and it nearly killed me so it is illogical they are relevant to my deeds and it is irrelevant if they are pleased or displeased about my purpose and so in turn they have been reduced to an obstacle that pattern detection and pondering is required to negate. The scribes have this concept in their head that their opinion matters but their opinion only matters to them. When one suggests the scribes are simply obstacles the scribes will start their elementary logic about: "That is not nice to say" or "That is not healthy to look at scribes as obstacles" because the scribes perceive their opinions matters to anyone but their self. The scribes seek to matter because they do not matter, they seek purpose because they have no purpose, they seek relevance because they have no relevance. The scribes in seeking harmony only achieve greater disharmony and this creates great suffering and that great suffering creates their desire to seek harmony and only achieves greater disharmony. This is all relative to the concept of a house built on the sand will crumble when the storms arrive.

[Is that so?" was all he would say.] This is a house built on rock and a house that does not crumble when the storms arrive. The scribes have all the laws and all the armies and perceive they are wise to push the education on the innocent children and their judges say that is proper and they have a right to do that to children and my only response to that is : Is that so?

61

7:08:47 PM – A depressed or suicidal person on the surface appears to be doing something they are not doing. A suicidal person is a person that has infinite intelligence but they have been turned down to about 10% mental ability and they are in fact attempting to fix their self and they understand subconsciously what is required to fix their self, and that is to defeat their fear of death, but because they are turned down to 10% cerebral ability because of the education they do not always "fix" their self. All a suicidal person is doing unknowingly on a conscious level is attempting to defeat their fear of death and that is the remedy to unveil their right brain but because they are mentally hindered by the education they often literally die. This is why the education is putting human beings at a mental disadvantage and often killing them but never ever making any of them wise but instead making them stupid or out of touch with reality or their own perceptions. This is an indication what happens when you push left brain favoring education on the delicate developing mind of a six year old child. So we have a human being that has their right brain traits veiled to a subconscious level as a result of all that left brain favoring education they got as a child and so a portion of those children attempt to fix their self and they are what the ones in alternative sense of time perception dimension call suicidal or depressed and they are what is known in no sense of time perception dimension as the meek and the poor in spirit. This means there are two completely alternative perception dimensions on a cerebral level happening in one consistent physical dimension at the exact same time. So what has happened is the being that got the education and have not applied the remedy are thus in sense of time alternate perception dimension and because they continue to give that same education to their own children they have a majority and so they are calling the shots for everyone so they have hijacked the physical dimension not intentionally but unknowingly. So subconsciously they are aware they are mentally hindering the children and they are aware they were mentally hindered as children subconsciously but that right brain signal is veiled so it is coming out backwards into their conscious state. So once they hear the truth relative to the education some have some redeemable qualities and can at least understand to a degree and when they figure out what is happening they go into depression and that is logical because that is an end stage or indication right brain is unveiling. So depression and suicidal people are simply people who are waking up from the neurosis caused by the education and everyone else is a fatality from the education and perhaps will never wake up. The problem with that is, the majority are fatalities so they will continue to put the children into the neurosis and they will seek to marginalize the depressed and suicidal. This is why the last thing Jonah said after assessing the situation is "Should I just kill them all?"

[Jonah 4:11 And should not I spare Nineveh, that great city, wherein are more than sixscore thousand persons that cannot discern between their right hand and their left hand; and also much cattle?]

This has nothing to do with political, economic, material aspects at all, or even belief systems. This has to do with the majority of the species is in deep neurosis because the majority of the species before them were in deep neurosis and decided to put them in deep neurosis and assumed that was a wise decision when in reality is was a stupid decision and that will never ever stop unless everything stops. The whole species has Ebola and every time they have a child they give that child Ebola so what is the solution?

[Jonah 4:11 And should not I spare..]

Should I kill all of them or should I not kill all of them? At first Jonah said kill me.

[Jonah 4:3 Therefore now, O LORD, take, I beseech thee, my life from me; for it is better for me to die than to live.]

Jonah said "Kill me", because he knew the solution was to kill them. A being of sound mind has something called a conscience and that is relative to right brain intuition and that is called a soul relative to these texts. Because they are of sound mind they are in harmony and harmony seeks harmony but Jonah was in a position where the solution was disharmony and he could not bring himself to accomplish the solution because he would have to use self control to achieve disharmony. Killing for a being that factually has no conscience, or right brain intuition is a piece of cake and killing others for a being that has a conscience is nearly impossible. The scribers will kill for sand, rocks, oil, tree's, water, food, money, drugs, pride, greed, envy, lust, sloth, control and the list goes on into infinity but a sound minded being cannot do that unless they are a god of concentration and self control which means they are not ever prone to kill others and that is why this whole situation has never been solved and perhaps will never be solved. Another way to look at it is Jonah knew even if he killed that entire city it would not solve the problem, he knew he would have to kill everyone in every city that got the education and did not apply the remedy and then totally outlaw reading, writing and math. Whoever wrote this comment, and it is totally irrelevant who did, already understood that [Genesis 2:17 But of the tree of the knowledge of good and evil, thou shalt not eat of it: for in the day that thou eatest thereof thou shalt surely die.]

It is a simply if/then statement. You get that reading, writing and math you die as a species and there are no exceptions or ways around that ever because applying the remedy is far too harsh for a human being to go through in a mentally hindered state of consciousness. You can read and write and use math but when you come to the understanding you have to mindfully kill yourself to an absolute scale to get back to how intelligent you were before you got that education you will understand what a problem is. Only a fool could apply the remedy the full measure and live to tell about it and so I say you are not a fool you are a fatality. That is a nice way of saying you cannot escape the death that education has made you. One might suggest you have intelligence as long as you never ever compare yourself to me. I suffer because I hope.

Because I suffer I hope.
I hope I suffer because.
Because I hope I suffer.
I hope I suffer because I hope.
I suffer because I hope I suffer.
I suffer I hope because I hope I suffer.

"Meditation in the midst of action is a thousand times stronger than meditation in stillness"
- Hakuin Ekaku, Zen Buddhist Master

The key word in the above comment is action. If one meditates in a safe location it is called taking a nap and if one meditates in a dark spooky place alone at night it is called applying the remedy. So it is not so much about the meditating, it is more about what actions are happening while one is meditating. Though I walk through the valley of a pleasant meadow I fear not, is nothing like though I walk through the valley of the shadow of death and fear not. Those who think about losing their life mindfully preserve it is not like those who lose their life mindfully preserve it. Meditating in the above comment is really just saying do not panic; fear not; deny one's self; submit; bow; yield mindfully in a situation with lots of perceived action. It is similar to the comment when everyone around you is losing their mind or in panic and you do not panic. The vast majority of scribes will run like scared dogs when the shadow of death arrives but the fool, the meek, the poor in spirit may not run. This is all relative to the fact in the sense of time perception dimension or in that extreme left brain state the hypothalamus is very sensitive and so the only way to remedy that is to get into a situation of great action and then deny the signals it is sending and a situation of perceived death is the most powerful signal one can get from the hypothalamus.

4/10/2010 4:46:23 PM -Depression: Depression is a disturbance in mood characterized by varying degrees of sadness, disappointment, loneliness, hopelessness, self-doubt, and guilt.

A right brain trait is ambiguity. Ambiguity = self-doubt relative to depression. So depression has a symptom called self doubt and self doubt is a symptom right brain traits are attempting to come to the surface and that right brain trait is ambiguity. So this shows depression is not depression it is an end stage that right brain aspects are coming back to the conscious state after education veils the right brain traits. There is no mention in the above definition of depression relative to sensitivity. That is a major factor because another right brain trait is intuition and that is what makes a depressed person so very sensitive or sentimental in a way, so as the ambiguity (self doubt) aspects starts to show so does the intuition and also the paradox and all of these aspects create the illusion of confusion simply because the person is not use to these aspects in the conscious state. It is not possible to be depressed when right brain is in the conscious state because its random access processing is simply far too fast. This of course goes with any emotion or state of mind: greed, lust, envy to name a few. It is simply a trait of right brain random access, the mind is pondering from one thought to another very swiftly so it is not relative to "how good a person is" it is just a trait of right brain random access. So this means depression itself can only ever be achieved to a prolonged degree in a person with right brain traits veiled to a subconscious state and that can only be achieved if a person gets lots of left brain favoring education and math. All of these symptoms [sadness, disappointment, loneliness, hopelessness, self-doubt, and guilt] are not possible in the machine state or in the now state of mind for prolonged periods, when right brain is unveiled because they are relative to coveting and also relative to attachment.

Sadness: feeling or showing unhappiness, grief, or sorrow.

[Exodus 15:14 The people shall hear, and be afraid: sorrow shall take hold on the inhabitants of Palestina.]

[and be afraid: sorrow shall take hold] = sadness; a symptom of depression.

These symptoms are symptoms of firstly fear. [sadness, disappointment, loneliness, hopelessness, self-doubt, and guilt]

Fear: an unpleasant feeling of anxiety or apprehension caused by the presence or anticipation of danger.

A person may eat lots of food and say I feel guilty but really they are afraid eating all that food will have unwanted consequences. Loneliness is the fear of being alone and that suggests anticipation of being alone and that suggests a time based awareness and that is not possible in the machine state. Another way to look at it is when right brain is unveiled it has so much ambiguity and paradox one cannot really relate to being alone as a "bad" thing. Loneliness is associated with being a bad thing but right brain does not deal well with absolutes only probabilities. It may be bad to be alone or it may be good to be alone and that is the minds final answer so this mindset of loneliness would never be achieved. If one looks at these depression symptoms and speeds them up to an extreme, as in one can be sad but only for about ten seconds relative to a clock then they can see how one would never really be sad they would be going through these states of mind so fast they would always be generally in neutral and this is relative to the quick and the slothful aspects. A state of depression denotes long periods of these mental states maintained and that could never happen with right brain throwing out random access thoughts at speeds based on seconds so this means depression itself is a symptom firstly that right brain is veiled and secondly that it is attempting to come back to the center or come back to the conscious state after the written education has veiled it. So society spends quite a bit of effort treating depression and so society spends quite a bit of effort treating a symptom caused by the written education so society is treating symptom's it is also creating and that is a form of vanity. Society is creating problems so it can solve those problems and that perhaps is an indication of some deep seeded boredom on a species level. This is relative to the concept of mankind is afraid of flat ground not mountains. On a species level if we are aware we have absolutely no purpose then it is logical we would be creating problems to solve to give off the impression of purpose. If on a species level we have this definitive purpose then it is not logical we would be creating problems to solve, we would be engaged in this progressive purpose instead but creating problems to solve suggests lack of progression. A person with a sense of time would see no purpose at all as very sad and that is exactly what a depressed person is going through, the self –doubt aspect. Self doubt in a way is a person that is aware there is no point and there is no purpose and nothing matters and in that extreme left brain state with the emotional capacity in a prolonged state that can lead to long periods of depression but in the machine state it is just a concept and not so much a emotionally sad aspect. One would not go to an alligator and say "Quit sunning yourself all day go be productive and have purpose." "Mr. Alligator get off your lazy butt and go apply yourself." The human species cannot agree on a purpose and that is an indication there may not be any purpose at all. We can agree we have to have offspring to continue the species but after that it pretty much all falls apart relative to purpose and that is a sad prospect for a being with a pronounced emotional capacity yet that is just a concept to a machine. If I suggest "I have no purpose" the very first thing a person with a sense of time will perhaps conclude is "He is depressed." But that is not a reflection on me that is a reflection on how they perceive things in that alternate sense of time perception dimension. I get this sense of no purpose because I do not perceive I accomplish anything and that is relative to right brain paradox not allowing my mind to perceive I am accomplishing anything and that is mentally healthy. If I write one book and my mind says "That's the greatest accomplishment in the world and you should be very tired and you need to rest because you wrote a book." that is mentally unhealthy because the body reacts to what the mind perceives. This is why the tribes were turned into slaves by the scribes because the tribes never perceived they were accomplishing anything mentally and so they made great "cash cows". Another way to look at it is in the machine state one does not perceive they accomplished something an hour ago and one does not perceive they are about to accomplish something in an hour so they are in a state of just doing with no consciousness awareness of what they have done or what they will do and this is the no sense of time mindset. So everything in the no sense of time perception dimension should seem odd to a person in the sense of time perception dimension because the two dimensions are complete alternates. Whatever a person in one dimension says to a person in the other dimension the truth relative to the initial person is perhaps the opposite. So the sense of time perception dimension is very achievement focused and so the reverse would be the no sense of time perception dimension would be purposeless or no achievement focused. Relative to you I may be achieving something but relative to me I am not achieving anything and that is logical since we are in alternate perception dimensions. I do not sense time and you do so the only possible reality since neither of us are on drugs or mind altering drugs is we are in altered states of consciousness and that is what a dimension is.

Dimension: a level of consciousness, existence, or reality.

So we are on different levels of consciousness without the use of drugs and so that means there can only be one normal level of consciousness and that means one of us has done something to alter their level of consciousness from the normal level of consciousness to the alternate abnormal level of consciousness. So in a true vacuum human beings are either in the sense of time perception dimension or the no sense of time perception dimension and so the fact reading, writing and math heavily favor the left brain aspects suggest it is probable that is what puts a person in the sense of time perception dimension. It is not as probable I was in normal sense of time perception dimension and did a one second mental exercise and then went to an alternate no sense of time perception dimension. It is more probable I left the alternate sense of time perception dimension caused by the education and returned to the normal no sense of time perception dimension because my mental clarity has increased and my cognitive ability has increased and that means it is not logical I would go to an abnormal perception dimension and my cerebral ability would increase because one is optimum in their natural habitat so to speak. Another way to look at it is, if a person has blinders on and then takes them off and then they can see much better it is logical the blinders were abnormal or a hindrance. I do not perceive people in the sense of time perception dimension are mentally ill as in parts of their brain are missing I perceive they are in an abnormal perception dimension so things are much harder for them to deal with because they are out of their normal perception element.

Behavior Disorders (Disruptive): All disruptive behavior is not the same, Behavior Disorders is an umbrella term that includes more specific disorders, such as Conduct Disorder, Oppositional Defiance Disorder, and ADHD.

This "disorder" is really just saying young children do not like to be told what to do because right brain which is still strong in children, likes to think for itself so treating this "disorder" is really just turning a person into a sheep. The child is not doing what an adult that is in extreme left brain state is telling them to do so clearly the child is at fault because it cannot be the adult is in an abnormal state of mind where they are a coveting control freak. Firstly we need to add control freak disorder.

Control freak disorder: A being conditioned into an extreme left brain state of mind and when their directions are ignored they automatically assume it is because the person they gave directions to has a behavior disorder.

If person A tell persons B what to do and person B resists and then person A determines that person has a mental disorder that is in fact a fear tactic to get person B to do what person A wants them to do." If you don't do what I say you are evil and mentally ill." That is a god complex. Person A assumes they are the end all be all relative to giving directions so anyone that does not follow their directions must be evil or bad or mentally ill. That is a symptom the ambiguity aspect of person A's mind, a right brain trait, is absent from their perception. A sound minded human being would have self doubt relative to another person not doing what they suggest they should do. It is one thing to tell a person what to do and when they do not do it to just assume your argument was not convincing enough and it is another thing to cram pills down that person's throat and call them mentally ill when they ignore your directions. The difference is one is making humble suggestions with no fear tactics attached and one is a control freak tyrant. If you want people to listen to your directions first convince them you are God and if you are unable to do that then you need to work on your mental capabilities because if you cannot convince people you are God then they perhaps they are wise not to listen to your directions to begin with and so you should not punish them for ignoring you by cramming pills down their throat.

Behavior Disorders (Disruptive):

Disruptive: interrupting usual order or progress.

Usual: characteristic or expected of somebody or something.

[usual order or progress] is assuming there is a usual order or progress so right off the bat this word is totally relative. Usual order relative to what? "Usual order" is a fear based concept just like "disrupting the peace" and just like "law abiding citizen."

Law: a rule of conduct or procedure recognized by a community as binding or enforceable by authority.

There have been moments in our history where the law said harm certain people and the authorities enforced that law so the concept of law abiding itself is a dangerous absolute. Suggesting you are potentially a law abiding citizen is more realistic.

Law abiding citizen = a sheep than does not question or doubt authority and thus one is prone to do follow that law if their right brain ambiguity and intuition are veiled.

Potentially law abiding citizen = a person that firstly thinks for their self and is thus a threat to any control structure.

[Luke 22:33 And he said unto him, Lord, I am ready to go with thee, both into prison, and to death.] This comment is saying this being is willing to break the law if it does not agree with his sensibilities and he is willing to be put in prison and also willing to die because thinking for yourself is paramount because in this narrow there are many illusion and traps ripe with fear tactics.

Oskar Schindler said that exact comment in his own way and put it to practice. Oskar said in a way "I am ready to go with thee, both into prison, and to death." If he was caught doing what he did he would have been put into prison or killed. So this whole concept of "I am a law abiding citizen" is a peer pressure fear tactic.

Law: a rule of conduct or procedure recognized by a community as binding or enforceable by authority.

Rule: an authoritative principle set forth to guide behavior or action.

A law is a rule. Think about school. Who is the authority in your class room? The teacher. There is no difference between a teacher and a police officer relative to traditional education. If you drop a piece of trash on the road a police officer will perhaps punish you with a ticket or jail and if you misspell a word on a test a teacher will punish you with a bad grade. If a police officer arrests you for breaking a rule which is a law, that will stay with you and affect you for the rest of your life and if a teacher gives you enough bad grades that will also stick with you the rest of your life so the common thread is, if you follow the rules you are rewarded by not being punished. So what that means is in a control structure punishment itself is an understood unless proved otherwise by following the rules. Following the rules is not second nature so in order to get people to follow the rules they must use fear tactics.

If everyone just followed every rule naturally there would be no need for any control structure so this is an indication perhaps that the control structure is abnormal. The control structure will always use fear logic to convince a person prone to fear of the value of rules and laws. If one considers the tribes in the Amazon they have no education or math and they also would not get near civilization with a ten foot pole. They perhaps do not have any laws or rules at all; other words everything is dealt with as it arises. This means there is no list of rules and laws one has to follow and so they are able to adapt readily to any situation. Just by looking at the spirit of the definition of a rule one can perhaps detect the strong control aspect.

[an authoritative principle set forth to guide behavior or action.]

Authoritative: convincing, reliable, backed by evidence, and showing deep knowledge.

[showing deep knowledge.] Knowledge is just information without wisdom.

[to guide behavior] = to control behavior = tyranny

Tyranny: cruelty and injustice in the exercise of power or authority over others.

If a teacher tells a small child they are stupid indirectly by giving them a poor grade on a spelling test that is cruelty and also and exercise of power or authority over another. The deeper reality is someone is controlling the behavior of that teacher and telling that teacher how to exert their authority over the children so that teacher is also under control. So then we have a school superintendent and they answer to the state school board and they answer to the parents of that state so the parents of that state are in fact indirectly telling that teacher to be cruel to their own children by exercising authority over their own children to guide(control) that child's behavior and when that child resist they call it a [Behavior Disorders (Disruptive)] and cram pills down that child's throat: Are you starting to understand why the wise beings in the ancient texts sacrificed their lives so they could explain the remedy so you could restore your right brain traits after the education veiled them so you would not go through life as a blind sheep?

You think the teacher or the police officer or the government is harming the children but in reality since you cannot see more than one step ahead you do not have the foresight which comes with having random access processing to see you are the one harming the children. The government doesn't control you, you control them, the police don't control you, you control them, the teacher doesn't control you, you control them, so if anyone is harming the children it is you. The government and the police and the teachers do not pass any laws or rules unless the people say it is okay and that means you passed and allowed the compulsory education law so you harm your own children and when your children start acting very strange and abnormal all you can say is "I do not know what happened to my child." Your children were not depressed until you got a hold of them and they were not ashamed and they were not embarrassed and they were not greedy and they were not lustful until you got your hands on them and attempted [to guide behavior]. The children are not what you say, they are what you are. You are ashamed, embarrassed, depressed and afraid and so the children are the same, so the problem is around your two feet; how about the psychologists are the problem not the children. How about the control freaks are the problem not the children. Perhaps that is very infinitely beyond your mental capacity to grasp. I understand one thing clearly. In order to communicate with you I must put myself in your shoes and when I do that it harms me. I have to become what is going on in your mind and when I do that I become you for a moment and it harms me and so I lash out just as you lash out. I have to assume the role of the cursed in order to communicate with the curse and it harms me. Just thinking what you are thinking harms me. I have to go back into the place of sorrow where you are at in order to communicate with you because you cannot relate to where I am at from the place of sorrow where you are. I have to go back into hell just so I can attempt to talk to you. I prefer to just go away and leave you there but I am compelled to attempt to communicate with you because I know you would do the same for me. You would not abandon me in the place of sorrow so I will not abandon you. I will now discuss something or importance. - 7:57:03 PM

Fool's think they have plenty of two things: time and good advice.

4/11/2010 12:11:38 AM – The middle way concept in Buddhism is relative to the comment about a house divided cannot stand and relative to the comment about a house built on the sand cannot stand the storms. The written education favors left hemisphere and thus does not favor right hemisphere so the mind becomes unsound and thus the mind falls out of the middle way, and so the fruits of the being exhibit symptoms of that. Once the mind falls out of the middle way or harmony everything else follows. Disharmony seeks disharmony and perceives disharmony is harmony. The fruits of the tree are a symptom of the tree and if the tree is rotten or unsound then the fruits will be rotten or unsound. These are elementary understandings. It is logical a being that has fallen out of the middle way, mental harmony will not be able to correct that knowingly unless they go against the grain of their nature relative to their state of mind because the grain relative to an unsound mind is disharmony and so one is not prone to find harmony in a state of disharmony unless they go against their nature in that unsound state of mind. This is relative to the concept of deny yourself. Deny yourself is going against the grain of yourself and so that would suggest "yourself" is in a disharmony state and the only way to negate that or remedy that is to deny that state. This is not hocus pocus, pixie dust or lizard men, this is simply what must happen once the mind is bent to an unsound state by the years of left brain favoring written education. One must be in a mindset of humility before they will ever attempt to correct a situation. Once a being determines it is possible all that left brain favoring education could have caused unwanted mental side effects on them they have started a pondering process which leads to further understandings. This is what is known as being open-minded. One is open-minded if they can consider there very well may have been some unwanted mental side effects caused by the education they received as a child due to the fact their frontal lobe aspects do not develop until they are in the twenties. Ambiguity and knowing are the two different paths. Ambiguity can lead to questions and experimentation and belief can lead to isolation.

[Half my friends have chosen to stay home and raise their kids, and (they are) beautiful and (educated) women.] = Beauty = popular; educated = popular; demotic = written language and means popular.

4/9/2010 1:24:00 PM - "Follow me into the desert as thirsty as you are."- Soundgarden – Song: Burden in my Hand

4/12/2010 7:01:58 PM – There is a story about passover. The concept is any person that put blood on their door were passed over and anyone who did not were paid a visit by this "spirit" and that spirit brought death to their first born. The blood on the door represented sacrifice. The remedy is sacrifice. The scribes have aversions to many things because in that extreme left brain state they see parts. One that see's parts is prejudice because not matter what they are pleased with there is always going to be something to compliment that. They are pleased with displeasure, they are pleased with prejudice, of course this is because they were conditioned into such an extreme left brain state they have no choice but to have this prejudice aspect because that is a left brain trait, seeing parts. So the blood on the door represented sacrifice which means people in that house kept the covenant and applied the fear not remedy in one form or another. So this blood on the door was in some way similar to the fish the true early Christians used to show directions to the meeting spot. The blood on the door would seem rather strange to the scribes. The scribes have aversions and especially aversion to things like blood and death and because of this no scribe would put blood on their door because it would perhaps not be too popular. So this blood on the door meant when the ones came into the city to attack the scribes their house was passed over. This concept is very similar to the reality in World War 2 the allies had these little clickers and when they saw someone approach at night they would click on the clicker and if the person that approached did not click their clicker it meant they were the enemy and they were attacked. So this blood on the door was an act a scribe would not likely participate in because they had many aversions to things, like blood on a door. So the blood on the door was something a scribe would not put on their door and even if they were told to put blood on their door they would not do it because it would seem very "wrong" or "bad" or "evil". That made a perfect way to make sure the ones who were attacking the city that night would not attack their own "kind" or the kindred, the ones who did keep the convent by applying the remedy after getting the written education. The deeper readily is there were factually no tribes living in cities, tribes being human beings that did not get the education or math at all, unless they were slaves of the scribes in the cities. Granted you may perceive there is some spirit going from door to door attacking anyone who did not have the blood on the door and that would be an accurate determination as long as one understands a human being that applies the remedy has the spirit of God, the right brain, the image of God in man on their side, so they are "filled" with the spirit, and in that relation there were spirits going from door to door attacking the ones who did not apply the remedy and that would be indicated because they did not have blood on their door. Be mindful God has no prejudice and no aversions [Genesis 1:10 And God called the dry land Earth; and the gathering together of the waters called he Seas: and God saw that it was good.]

[and God saw that it was good.] = No aversions or prejudice = everything is one thing = a holistic outlook, a right brain trait.

For example if I had true hatred or prejudice against the scribes I certainly would not be writing books explaining to them the most powerful understandings relative to mankind since the invention of written language and math which is the remedy to negate the unwanted mental side effects cause as a result of learning written language and math. So on one hand I am selling out to the adversary but that is required because I have no prejudice and that means I am not a good judge relating to what scribes will understand this remedy and apply it and some scribes will hear this remedy and mock it. Every scribe gets the benefit of my doubt. It is far too complex to determine who will hear the remedy and apply it and who will not apply it after hearing the remedy. Sometimes a person will hear the remedy and mock it but that only means they are pondering it on a subconscious level. Sometimes a person will hear the remedy and say "Yes that is truth it is wise" and then after a period of time relative to a calendar they will forget about it and never think about it again. Some that hear the remedy are on fire for the remedy but soon they forget about it and never apply it and sometimes ones that mock the remedy slowly come to realize its importance and end up applying it. Sometimes a scribe will hear the remedy and mock it but then when they are in a situation in life that is difficult or makes them sad or depressed the remedy comes back into their thoughts and they see it in a different light. This is why the testimony is so important because one will never be intelligent enough to determine how the scribes will react to it on a scale of time. The ancient texts suggest probabilities relative to who are blessed or chosen relative to the scribes who would make good candidates for the remedy. "Blessed are the poor in spirit" and "the meek shall inherit the earth."

Meek: showing submissiveness and lack of initiative or will.

Submissiveness: giving in or tending to give in to the demands or authority of others(the kindred, the ones with no sense of time who have applied the remedy)

One perhaps can see why the doctrine in Islam is submit. Show submissiveness. This is a state of mind a scribe has to be in order to "seek the shadow of death and then fear not" This submissive state of mind is the where one has to be mentally in order to lose their life mindfully or to deny their self the full measure. These ancient texts are flawless in their explanations relative to the remedy to the written education but the catch is, they are very complex and if one gets the education they have their right brain complexity silenced or veiled so it is logical these ancient texts would go right over their heads so to speak. One way to look at it is I accidentally restored the complexity thought processes and so these texts are flawless relative to me in their explanations but to a scribe, a person who has not applied the remedy they factually will never be able to grasp these texts, because they are written or dictated by beings that had complexity in their thought processes. These ancient texts are elementary cause and effect relationships relative to the written education neurosis and simple to understand but if one has their right brain complexity and pattern detection veiled they will not be able to understand these texts in a billion years and so far the scribes have not understood them at all in 5400 years and that trend will never stop until they restore their right brain traits. The scribes cannot understand what they are not capable of understanding. Another way to look at it is a human being needs all their senses to understand these texts and some of those senses are pattern detection, complexity and intuition and if any of these senses are even slightly veiled or hindered it is not going to happen for them. This reality is relative to the comment "They hear but do not understand". The scribes do not have all their senses at full power namely right brain pattern detection, intuition and complexity because the tree of knowledge, written education favors left brain so much it veils those right brain aspects. This in fact is logical and in fact is perhaps not supernatural. If one has their right hand cut off they will have trouble picking up things. So now I am in a position I am explaining things no being in recent history has ever explained to you in such detail and you are assuming I am special or gifted or wise and when I suggest I simply accidentally applied the remedy to restore my right brain traits after written education veiled said traits, you may assume I am meek and you will simply come to wrong conclusions and assume I am going to lead you or direct you or save you and that factually is not going to be happening. Our species got ourselves into a very deep pit with the written education and we are showing no signs or getting out of that mental pit we are in and so if you can convince me there is any problem in this universe more pressing than addressing this written education induced neurosis reality I will bow before you. The secondary problem or pattern I have detected is the scribes only understand one thing very well and that is violence. Non-violence is great as long as it works, to paraphrase Malcolm X.

Adversary: an opponent in a conflict, contest, or debate.

Opponent: somebody who plays, fights, or competes against you in a contest.

I am in a contest with you whether you want to be in a contest with me or not and I have no rules, morals or class so you would be infinitely wise to adopt that same strategy or I will defeat you soundly.

Defeat: to win a victory over a competitor.

So if one reverses this concept,[Meek: showing submissiveness and lack of initiative or will], they will come up with words like pride, arrogant, egotistical.

This definition of arrogant : feeling or showing self-importance and contempt or disregard for others. Arrogance is a good indication of the two contrary dimensions this education has put us in as a species. Everything applies differently to each perception dimension. For example the scribes knowingly or unknowingly show [contempt or disregard for others] namely children when they push all that left brain education on the young children because it hinders that child's mind, so they are very arrogant but they assume they are wise to do that to the children because they truly believe written education and math on an absolute scale is : [Genesis 3:6 ...a tree to be desired to make one wise] when in fact if not taught properly or taught to children at a very young age whose mind to does not even develop until they are in the twenties, ruins the child's mind on an absolute scale.

Now relative to me, I also [show contempt or disregard for others], namely scribes, because I believe they mentally harm children with their "brand" of education and then they do not even have the foresight to explain the remedy to restore the child's mind, and they also do not even explain there may perhaps be some unintended mental consequences with the education considering it is all left brain favoring. So I appear self righteous or arrogant but that is fine with me because I have no morals, class, pride, ego and so one can announce to the universe I explained I have no morals , class or pride and I am certain my blood pressure will not rise one degree. You can say whatever you wish about me and I will continue to work on my argument that the scribes mentally hinder the children with their wisdom education and we can both come to the understanding of who will be left standing when I get warmed up to 1%. These words mean nothing to me because they are all based on absolutes and that is not how things work in this narrow. This narrow has paradox and complexity and there are very few situations where an absolute applies, yet all words are perhaps based on absolutes.

"I am good and you are bad." If a scribe says that, relative to the no sense of time perception dimension they are saying "I am bad and you are good." Perhaps the scribes are good at mentally hindering all the children with their wisdom education and perhaps they are bad at not mentally hindering all the children with their wisdom education but even at that, they are not absolutely good at it because I escaped the mental hindering so perhaps they are just very good at mentally hindering the children but not absolutely good at mentally hindering all the children with their wisdom education. I am in the no sense of time perception dimension so when I say to a scribe "Thank You." what do you think I mean? Now a scribe will say "That is very evil to say thank you and perhaps mean the reverse." But the scribes are control freaks and they never quite grasp a human being can think anything they want to think and do anything they want to do relative to developing their mind and their mental fortitude and the beings around them have absolutely no bearing or ability to control that mental exercising. The whole point of rule and laws is to control a person's behavior and that is the same as saying controlling what a person thinks. It is logical if a person says something contrary to how they want a person to think they will attempt elementary fear or scare tactics. "You are evil if you think that or say that." That perhaps works on being with 10 percent mental capacity but that is laughable for being in the no sense of time perception dimension because beings in that dimension are fully aware of exactly what the scribes are thinking on a conceptual basis at all times. That a nice way to say I was once in the sense of time perception dimension , (blind) but now I am in the no sense of time perception dimension(I can see) and I factually understand your sense of time perception dimension far better than you perhaps ever will because I have something you currently do not have, and that is contrast. I am looking at the sense of time perception dimension from the outside or from a position of hindsight and the scribes do not have that luxury and that have never been to my perception dimension since they were tiny children, the no sense of time dimension so they are clueless to it ways also, so they do not understand their own dimension very well and they have no clue about the dimension I am in, so they are essentially in a position where they are so outclassed it is as if I should feel sorry for them because they stand absolutely no chance. The only solution the scribes have since they are outclassed on every level in a cerebral and logical way is violence. A bully tends to be quick to judge and quick to resort to violence and thus slow to understand that is their nature. Disharmony cannot go against its nature so it will say "I am doing a good thing" when in reality it is a destructive thing. That trend cannot change unless disharmony denies itself or its nature. This means the meek which are the suicidal and depressed and are attempting to deny their nature and once in a while one accomplishes it without literally killing their self and they return to harmony.

[Mark 8:34 ..., he said unto them, ..., let him deny himself,..]

So Jesus would come up to you in your sense of time perception state of mind and say "Deny yourself." And you would become offended and say harsh things to him and spit on him and mock him and say "You are not so wise and special because you are telling me to deny myself" and Then Jesus would say "Go mindfully lose your life to preserve your life." and you would say "You are arrogant and egotistical and crazy and stupid and self righteous." And that is exactly what the scribes said about him and that is exactly why they butchered him, he was infinitely beyond the mental ability of the scribes to understand in their hindered state of mind, the scribes saw truth as lies, wisdom as foolishness, clarity as insanity simply because insanity can only see sanity as insanity unless insanity becomes meek and meek means submissive. That's a nice way to say I am not asking for your opinion I am just telling you reality and you can spend the rest of your life attempting to grasp it. I understand things you do not know and I have determined to tell you said understandings and there is nothing you can do about it.

X = Sense of time perception dimension.
Y = No sense of time perception dimension.
(X) state of perception is caused by all the left brain favoring education.
(Y) state of perception is the state of perception one is in when they are born and the state of perception after one applies the remedy to the (X) state of mind perception.

X beings see parts.

Y beings see holistically. This suggests contrary perception dimensions. Things that apply in one dimension do not apply in the other dimension and this is the rift or divide and that is logical when dealing with alternate dimensions. So this comment is attempting to explain this alternate perception dimension aspect.

[Isaiah 5:20 Woe unto them that call evil good, and good evil; that put darkness for light, and light for darkness; that put bitter for sweet, and sweet for bitter!]

[that call evil good, and good evil] This is suggesting absolute alternate perception dimensions.

[that put darkness for light, and light for darkness] This is suggesting absolute alternate perception dimensions.

[that put bitter for sweet, and sweet for bitter!] This is suggesting absolute alternate perception dimensions.

The topic of this comment is [Woe unto them] Who is them? The scribes. A scribe is a human being that got lots of that left brain favoring written education which in turn put them in an absolute alternate perception dimension and the only way they can escape that is to apply the remedy to one degree or another. There is no possible way to escape that alternate perception dimension except for the remedy but there are many ways one can apply the remedy but the principle of the remedy is the same no matter which way they apply it. A person can get into a physiological traumatic accident and that may work. A person can meditate in the right situation and that may work. The point is the remedy in principle is the same.

So the complexity for a being that escapes the (X) perception dimension is they have to attempt to bridge this absolute reverse perception rift or division. This is what you may know as reverse psychology. A parent will use reverse psychology on a small child because that child is in the (Y) perception dimension.

If I tell you to embrace every single rule and law relative to your perception as in rules that are not even really literal laws then all I will accomplish is pushing you further into dimension (X). Dimension (X), left brain state, loves rules and directions so in (Y) dimension, with right brain unveiled, it is logical one would not like rules and directions, only because in (Y) state of mind a person learns from "mistakes" as well as "victories" and so there are not really any mistakes or victories only things to achieve further understandings. There is a paradox aspect that suggests I cannot actually lose or win no matter what strategy I use. For example, If I say follow every rule and here are a thousand more you have to follow and you do, you will go further and further into extreme left brain and that eventually will lead to you mentally collapsing and entering a depressed or suicidal state and from there you have a chance once in the ninth circle of hell, treason, to escape. If I suggest let go of some of those rules you have and maybe let go of a great majority of these rules you have burned into your head that are not even really laws just rules you picked up, then you will start favoring right brain and that will also lead you to become depressed and suicidal and once you get to the 9th circle of hell, treason, you have a chance of applying the remedy. So my only purpose is to get you to go to the 9th circle of hell, treason and I can do it in any number ways effectively and so I may appear harsh or cruel but the absolute reality is I did not put you in hell to begin with the "wisdom" education did. I have to give you lots of chemotherapy and it may kill you but it has a slight chance of saving you and I am indifferent to either outcome because the results are not my business only giving you the chemotherapy is my business. You can pay the piper slowly or you can pay the piper swiftly but my purpose is to make sure you pay the piper. The piper wants his payment and I am just a clerk here to collect it. It is not logical I would hide these realities from you or water them down because then you may get the impression I try. The point is I am of sound mind and thus I am not pleased to put you in a situation that may factually kill you. Harmony does not seek disharmony so I must over compensate and attempt to scare you away because it may kill you once you get to the 9th circle of hell. I am telling you things that are going to make you reevaluate your entire life and you may become so depressed you may get all caught up in that depression and forget that depression is just a symptom your right brain is unveiling and so you may believe the depression is real and you may kill yourself when all I am suggesting is that you mindfully let go or mindfully kill yourself. I am not prone to harm my own species because I am in a sound mind state or a harmony state but I must harm people on a mental level in order to wake them up and so I must apply self control to achieve disharmony and on top of that that the pickings are rather slim anyway, so to speak.

4/12/2010 9:47:44 PM – Lateralization of brain function is relative to the signals from each hemisphere and how they impact the whole mind. The corpus callosum is the bridge between the two hemispheres. So it is understood the hemispheres are contrary mirror images. The hemispheres do not have redundant systems is one way to look at it. The main complexity is how can one go about determining if the signals from one hemisphere are factoring in equally in contrast to the other hemisphere.

X = left hemisphere signals
Y = right hemipshere signals
Z = curpus callosum
A = sound mind relative to both hemisphere signals are getting equal "say"
B = one hemispheres signals are stronger or have more "say" than the other = unsound mind

$((X + Z) = (Y + Z)) = A$. So this equation is how a sound mind operates.

$((X+Z) > (Y + Z) = B$. This is how the mind is after all the left brain favoring education and thus is the reason why the being has to apply the remedy to return to (A) state of mind.

So this lateralization of brain function is factually happening and that is elementary but the real question is how does one determine their lateralization is sound or in absolute harmony?

The answer is quite simple. When absence of fear is achieved an absolute lateralization relative to brain function is achieved.

[2 Timothy 1:7 For God hath not given us the spirit of fear;...but,.. of a sound mind.]

So harmony relative to lateralization of brain function is determined by the level of fear one has. As fear decreases lateralization in brain function gets closer to perfect harmony or closer to (A).

If a being is ashamed, afraid, shy, depressed, guilt ridden or has aversions to words then their lateralization is way out of harmony.

If a being is ashamed, afraid, shy, depressed, guilt ridden or has aversions to sounds or music then their lateralization is way out of harmony.

If a being is ashamed, afraid, shy, depressed, guilt ridden or has aversions to colors or pictures then their lateralization is way out of harmony.

This concept relates to many aspects and the aversions can go into great detail. One can have an aversion to people of certain skin color, certain beliefs systems, certain creeds. One can have an aversion to a messy house. One can have an aversion to being hygienic or have an aversion to being unhygienic. One can have an aversion to certain smells. One might say "I hate the smell of that cologne." and that is a symptom their lateralization is way out of harmony. The being may assume they have "taste" in certain words or certain music or certain smell but they do not, they have aversions to those things because they "see" way to many parts because the left brain "seeing parts" aspect is sending stronger signals to the corpus callosum than the right brain holistic or non prejudice aspect is sending. So this means in perfect mental harmony one should be indifferent to things like sounds, smells, pictures and perhaps even tastes. It is one thing to have an aversion to putting your hand on a hot stove but it is a symptom of being mentally unsound to have an aversion to a picture of a hot stove, for example. If someone says "Hot stove" and you cringe in terror something is seriously wrong with the brain function lateralization. If someone says what you call a cuss word and you react mentally to that word any other way but indifferently then something is serious wrong with your brain function lateralization. I was watching a show about a police officer who was in court because he taserd a person and the police officer was giving his take on events and he started off his case by saying "The person was saying profanities to me." And then he repeated that and said "The person in question called me the F word and used many profanities." And it went on like this and the police officer continued to bring up the fact the main reason he taserd this being in part was because the person said a word that the police officer had been conditioned to have an aversion to. "It was proper that I literally physically harmed a person because that person was saying a word that I have an aversion to because as a child I got years of left brain favoring education pushed on my by law with no suggestions of its potentially bad mental side effects and now my brain function lateralization is completely out of harmony and it shows because I physically harmed a human being for making an inanimate sound I have an aversion to." I am using a police officer as an example but you are the exact same way. You pass laws to lock your own fellow citizens in jail for saying words. If you can come up with a better definition of an absolute mental abominated lunatic, call. The only thing I understand is I love spitting blood into my diaries.

When absence of fear is achieved an absolute lateralization relative to brain function is achieved. The complexity in this comment is fear. Fear is really an aversion.

Aversion : a strong feeling of dislike of somebody or something.

Smells, sounds, pictures, tastes, ideas. This should not be confused with an aversion to pain. People are not really afraid of pain they just have an aversion to it in most cases. A word, picture, or sound is not going to cause you physical pain but of course since you are anal retentive I will suggest sounds at very high decibels will cause physical pain. A picture of nudity will not cause you physical pain and that is indicated here when two beings that did not yet get the written education were nude.

[Genesis 2:25 And they were both naked, the man and his wife, and were not ashamed.]

So shame is an aversion and aversion is relative to fear or fear is relative to an aversion and after all that left brain favoring education ones lateralization is way out of harmony so they have aversions to many things and that means the remedy in part is to start working on all these aversions. If one has an aversion to a picture of nudity and they stare at the picture until they are indifferent to it then they no longer have an aversion to it. This same concept works with words, and tastes, and sounds and is relative to the concept of denying one's self. Now some "religious" scribes will say a picture of nudity is evil and that only proves they still have aversions and that proves they have not applied the remedy and that also proves if they could ever figure out what the tree of knowledge is I will remind them. Perhaps my lack of prejudice simply means I am infinitely self righteous so now you can stop invading my privacy and stop reading my private diaries. Perhaps if any being in this narrow was worth their salt they would have proved it by now. I am picking a fight with the scribes although they may be to mindfully retarded to grasp that. Some hear the truth and get angry because they do not want to admit they got beguiled to the infinite degree as children. In order to convince a blind man blindness is abnormal one must convince the blind man of the symptoms of blindness. Depression itself is impossible when right brain is at 50% and in the conscious state because its random access thought processing is so fast one simply can never maintain one state of mind for even a minute relative to a clock. So one may conclude that every person that has killed their self because of depression is a symptom they got that education and never applied the remedy and that would mean we have become a self harming species.

Freud said "Neurosis is the inability to tolerate ambiguity" and Roger Sperry a neurobiologist and Nobel prize winner said " What it comes down to is modern society discriminates against right hemisphere". If one combines those two comments knowing ambiguity is a right brain trait. What it comes down to is that modern society, the neurotics, discriminate against right brain traits like ambiguity by way of their left brain favoring education taught to the children improperly and at far too young of an age. Dyslexia is simply right brain random access figuring into the thought processes, so people who are dyslexic tend to have right brain unveiled to a degree and of course are considered mentally ill by society. Knowledge without pattern detection is just data and knowledge with pattern detection is wisdom. I am not saying you sold your soul, conscience, intuition (a right brain trait) when they(the scribes) forced you to eat off that tree of knowledge even though I just did. No being knows his character until they understand the truth.

4/13/2010 5:47:29 PM – [Luke 10:3 Go your ways: behold, I send you forth as lambs among wolves.]

[among wolves] = the scribes, the ones in sense of time perception dimension, the ones with right brain traits veiled so they have greatly hindered cognitive ability, the ones that mentally hinder the children with their wisdom education unknowingly and then assume they are wise for doing so, the ones that resort to violence because they are no longer mentally viable beings. You can pick and choose which description you like the best because they are all the same.

[I send you forth as lambs] This comment shows Jesus was aware of what he was sending these beings who did apply the remedy into. John the Baptist also knew what he was sending Jesus into when he assisted Jesus with his version of the remedy using water or baptism. Simply put sound minded human beings are docile because they have great cerebral capacity and they are not all caught up in control aspects like control over others and control over resources they are essentially non violent in nature and so that means the ones that sense time that are in alternate perception dimension are very prone to be violent. Jesus was saying to the few that did listen to him and applied the remedy, "I am sorry you are going to get slaughtered by the mental abomination scribes but that is the way it goes in this narrow." The only beings that don't get slaughtered that applied the remedy are the ones that never really applied the remedy the full measure. They are trapped in the fear dimensions still and so they will suggest everything in the universe except exactly what is on their mind so they still have much hesitation. One does not concern their self with the understood reactions of the lunatic scribes to the suggestion the written education and math hinders the mind. The lunatic scribes do not matter, is another way to look at it. The lunatic scribes are mentally destroying children on an industrial scale with their "wisdom" education and they do not even believe they are so they are irrelevant. You give your testimony and if they try to stop you by force, you remember you have freedom of speech and you have the right to defend yourself and you have the right to defend your children. I am mindful I am sending you into a frenzy of insane wolves by telling you to apply this remedy but that is the way it goes in this narrow.

This is the only prayer you are going to while you are applying the remedy and after you apply the remedy [Jonah 4:3 Therefore now, O LORD, take, I beseech thee, my life from me; for it is better for me to die than to live(in hell surrounded by lunatic scribes that mentally destroy the children on an industrial scale).] so you better get your priorities in order swiftly. The rules of the scribes is to mentally hinder all the children starting at the age of six so obviously their rules do not apply and are invalid and are rules of lunatics. Do you follow the rules of lunatics?

X = money : Y = food and water : Z = education : A = punishment : $X + Z = Y$: X without $Z = A$

Money is a false measure of popularity and a means to get food and water and if anyone does not follow the narrow rules to get it they are punished and deemed criminal. The problem is everyone needs food and water, so the power structure has a monopoly on food and water and so therefore they can manipulate behavior based on that. You did not go to school to get wise, you went to school so you could get food and water and in doing that you had your mind taken from you. It's simply a carrot and stick tactic.

More education = more luxury is the carrot

More education = more popularity

Demotic = written language and means popularity

demotic = demonic

The concept of selling your soul to the devil revolves around selling your soul for popularity.

demotic = written education = popularity = veils your right brain = kills your right brain intuition = intuition is your "soul"

Your intuition is your eyes it keeps you from being a sucker relative to having the wool pulled over your eyes = education blinds your eyes, right brain intuition

Intuition and right brain pattern detection are one of the senses we have to keep us alert and safe, but education turns those senses off so then one cannot think for their self and one is thus reduced to a "sheep".

How are right brain traits turned off? the 3 R's: reading, writing and arithmetic -- the domain and strength of the left brain

The more left brain is favored the more right brain is turned down; then attach punishments for doing poorly at the 3 R's and rewarding ones who do well at the 3'rs and it is a perfect brain washing structure.

Rewards for doing well at the 3 r's is popularity, water and food; so the concept of "one has a choice" is an illusion because everyone needs food and water and food and water are attached to the education.

[Jeremiah 8:8 How do ye say, We are wise, and the law of the LORD is with us? Lo, certainly in vain made he it; the pen of the scribes is in vain.] = when everything is said and done, all we are really doing is putting everyone to sleep. How can we say education is making one wise when it veils their right hemisphere to a subconscious state?

Think about this comment:

[On Sunday, militants planted explosives in a boys' school in Mohmand Agency, bringing to 40 the number of schools they have destroyed in the area, authorities said.No one was hurt in the attack.]

Why would any human being in a war blow up a school? It serves no military value. So this means something that is taught at that school is being stopped by blowing up that school. It has nothing to do with killing people. There are no military targets in a school. The only logical explanation is those schools were teaching this [the 3 R's: reading, writing and arithmetic -- the domain and strength of the left brain]. It makes no sense to blow up a school unless that school is not really a school but a factory that hinders the mind of children; a boot camp. That makes sense and that makes that "school" a valid military target. In this war of the minds so to speak, that school is just like a training camp. It is valid to bomb the enemies training camps in any conflict. That is logical in a conflict to bomb the enemies training camps and camps the enemy uses to make more soldiers. What appear to be happening is not happening. Human beings do not blow up schools, but human beings do blow up the adversaries training camps.

[bringing to 40 the number of schools they have destroyed in the area] This comment is not saying the militants blew up 40 schools it is saying the militants blew up 40 training camps of the adversary. Some of your most valuable senses have been turned off by the education namely pattern detection and intuition, right brain traits. You will perceive the militants are blowing up elementary schools with no one in them and it appears very strange or pointless considering they are outnumbered a million to one to begin with, but it is logical they would attack the enemies training camps no matter how outnumbered they were. One thing you have to remember at all times is that although the militants seem fanatical or hardcore I assure you the beings that have applied the remedy and speak , and write and explain the remedy are infinitely more hardcore because they create far more warriors than the militants ever will. You may perceive I am peaceful because I sit in my isolation chamber and write my thoughts down and never harm anyone physically but I assure you I make all militants look like peaceful beings and my middle name is fanatic relative to my determination to expose the scribes for what they are. And expose what the written education does to the mind of a child. Something along the lines of the pen is more effective than the sword but the catch is one has to be able to communicate with the scribes properly and if they can do that the sword becomes meaningless. The scribes did not kill John the Baptist, Jesus and the disciples and untold numbers of others, because they were violent, they killed them because the scribes could not argue with what they were saying relative to the remedy. The remedy works every time it is applied properly.

[Mark 1:22 And [they(scribes) were astonished at his doctrine]: for he taught them as one that had authority, and not as the scribes.]

The deeper reality is there are no absolutes in this war. I am compelled to write infinite books which means I am not compelled to be violent but that is my orders and I go with the flow so my orders are not absolute and my orders are not necessarily going to be your orders but I can suggest focus on the log in your eye after you apply the remedy because you may find communicating with the scribes is perhaps a more effective strategy in dealing with them. I do not have to be violent because I am mindful I can perhaps defeat the scribes meaning get them to adjust or question their education methods with my words. If I am unable to do that then it was not meant to be and understanding that means I will have gained an understanding and an understanding is perhaps all one can gain from life anyway. I do not judge what other beings that have applied the remedy do, but at times I do jab them a bit to let them know I am mindful of them. The ones that have applied the remedy have only one objective, to get the scribes to understand the education does hinder the minds of the children, and one might suggest the ones that have applied the remedy after 5400 years their patience is wearing thin. Only the ones who have not applied the remedy the full measure have mercy on the scribes. It is factually possible to explain this education situation to the scribes so they understand it but that does not mean they apply the remedy and that does not mean they will cease to mentally hinder the children but that is something of value or something of what you would call hope or progress. As a species we are really just fighting each other with words or with weapons and so I attempt to distance myself from that and write to myself to work on the log in my eye and that way I can ponder the patterns I detect from this war and seek a solution or at least come to further understandings. This war relative to the written education is a 5000 year old war so it is what you would call a stalemate. The scribes have the numbers but they do not have "eyes" to see their adversary. The ones that have applied the remedy, are not beaten and in fact only get better and better. So these "schools" on both sides are in fact "boot camps" and the complexity comes into play when one factors in the different perception dimensions. One camp has the beings that have applied the remedy and have right brain on their side so they either teach children oral education and very heavy long term memory education to keep right brain unveiled so they are aware of the dangers of traditional education. The scribes are not aware of the dangers of written education so it is logical they would not see their schools as "boot camps". One can look at it like if you take a six year old child and throw lots of left brain education on them with punishments and rewards attached to their performance in education then you are brainwashing, indoctrinating or thought controlling that child. Now if you do not push that education on the child you leave their mind intact and no matter what one tells that child it is very probable that child will think for their self because they will have the right brain intuition in the conscious state of mind and this means they will not make a very good soldier. This is what is happening with the militants and this is why they appear disorganized and contrary to that the scribes are very organized and have a very clear control structure. When it comes down to it they are human beings killing each other over this 5000 year old invention so it is very odd perhaps but that does not mean either side see's it that way and at the end of the day the children are the ones that lose on both sides. Humans got into this very strange habit of teaching children and that perhaps is a huge misstep. The adults want the children to think what they think and that leads to stagnation because the next generation should be seeking to avoid thinking what the last generation thought and that gives off the impression of progression or evolution.

For example the scribes will say the militants want us to go back to the stone age but in reality the scribes have been ruining children's minds for 5000 years and not one single thing has changed relative to that so they are still in the stone age. Five thousand year ago a scribe said "Come here child I will teach you to read and write and you will be wise." and today that exact thing is happening so that is not progression that is stagnation or what some say repeating the same thing over and over expecting different results. Written education and math and reading did not make you Einstein and it didn't make anyone you know Einstein and it's not going to make your children Einstein so what exactly is your goal in pushing all that left brain favoring education on a small innocent child whose mind does not even develop until they are twenty? It all comes down to this:

"What it comes down to is that modern society discriminates against the right hemisphere." - Roger Sperry (1973) Neurobiologist and Nobel Lauriat

How does modern society do that? With their left brain favoring boot camps they call school. You, your government, your leader and your god does not have the right to discriminate against the right hemisphere of a child. That's a fact and even if you do not think it is a fact you still are accountable for it. I have already decided on the solution. The scribes can mentally hinder all the children into infinity but I am going to continue to explain to the species that is what they are doing. This freedom of speech and freedom of press is my weapon and I am mindful the last thing in this universe the scribes are going to be doing is defending my right of freedom of speech and freedom of press. I will test your comments relative to "You will die to defend my right to say something." Are you going to die to defend my right to tell the species you knowingly or unknowing mentally hinder the children on an industrial scale starting at the age of six using written education? My intuition suggests you are not going to be dying to defend my right to tell the species these things.

I don't do drugs because I risk becoming enlightenment. In many ancient texts there are many contradictions and that is because the beings are attempting to use a language based on absolutes to explain concepts based on probabilities.

4/14/2010 5:52:06 PM - The darkness see's the light as darkness because the light reveals to the darkness what the darkness is.

4/15/2010 3:47:42 PM - "[Demotic (from Greek: δημοτικός dēmotikós, "popular") refers to either the ancient Egyptian script derived from northern forms of hieratic used in the Delta, or the stage of the Egyptian language following Late Egyptian and preceding Coptic. The term was first used by the Greek historian Herodotus to distinguish it from hieratic and hieroglyphic scripts. By convention, the word "Demotic" is capitalized in order to distinguish it from demotic Greek." – WIKIPEDIA.COM

This comment is suggesting the Greeks called Egyptian written language Demotic and that word means "popular".

Imhotep, means "the one that comes in peace".

"In priestly wisdom, in magic, in the formulation of wise proverbs; in medicine and architecture; this remarkable figure of Zoser's reign left so notable a reputation that his name was never forgotten. He was the patron spirit of the later scribes, to whom they regularly poured out a libation from the water-jug of their writing outfit before beginning their work." - James Henry Breasted – archeologist describing Imhotep.

[In priestly wisdom, in magic, in the formulation of wise proverbs] This may be suggesting a cult or the first cult of the "dark arts" namely a form of dimension travel.

[formulation of wise proverbs]
[He was the patron spirit of the later scribes, to whom they regularly poured out a libation from the water-jug of their writing outfit before beginning their work] I am certain this Imhotep is who this comment is referring to:

[Genesis 3:1 Now the serpent was more subtil than any beast of the field which the LORD God had made.]

[subtil] Is suggesting among other things crafty. This is suggesting crafty [In priestly wisdom, in magic, in the formulation of wise proverbs; in medicine and architecture] Architecture is crafty or a craft for example and also suggests labor or jobs.

[He was the patron spirit of the later scribes] This is a huge red flag. He was the patron "saint" of scribes or of script and this script relative to commonly used Egyptian hieroglyphics was called demotic. He was the Patron spirit of demotic. Demotic means popular so he was a patron Spirit of popularity and popularity is a symptom of pride and ego.

[He was the patron spirit of the later scribes] This is also suggesting Imhotep was the patron spirit of scribes and all of civilization or modern society is scribes or civilization teaches a form of script to everyone essentially so he is the "God" of civilization. It is logical since he was very big on script he would never speak poorly of it so it is logical if someone was suggesting there are problems with script he would respond with something like this:

[Genesis 3:3 But of the fruit of the tree which is in the midst of the garden, God hath said, Ye shall not eat of it, neither shall ye touch it, lest ye die.] So this comment is a being saying "do not use that tree of knowledge, that script, there is something wrong with it or some bad side effects caused by it.

[Genesis 3:4 And the serpent said unto the woman, Ye shall not surely die:] And this comment is Imhotep saying "No there is nothing wrong with it surly it is fine if I can do these things with it: [In priestly wisdom, in magic, in the formulation of wise proverbs; in medicine and architecture]"

[Genesis 3:5 For God doth know that in the day ye eat thereof, then your eyes shall be opened, and ye shall be as gods, knowing good and evil.] Then this line is a being saying "the problem with the script is it alters your perception so you start to see parts or have aversions or you become prejudice which is what knowing(perceiving) good and evil is.], and this is logical because [3 R's: reading, writing and arithmetic -- the domain and strength of the left brain]; left brain see's parts so if one does something that favors left brain enough they would start seeing parts or start having many prejudices which means [knowing good and evil.]

[Revelation 3:9 Behold, I will make them(the scribes) of the synagogue of Satan(Imhotep ; the patron spirit of scribes), which say they are Jews(believers of the ancient texts), and are not(because they never applied the remedy), but do lie(are false truth/ are in the reverse perception dimension); behold, I will make them to come and worship before thy feet(become submissive or meek by telling them the truth), and to know that I have loved thee.]

Imhotep means "the one who comes in, with peace"

[Luke 12:51 Suppose ye that I am come to give peace on earth? I tell you, Nay; but rather division:]

So Imhotep came in peace and it is logical the anti-scribes would come for division. This again suggests the two separate perception dimensions. So Imhotep is the patron saint of script and his "stand" is "I come in peace" and then Jesus speaking for the anti-scribes would logically come for division.

Simply put if the scribes are going to continue to mentally hinder the children by teaching the script improperly and never suggest the remedy to the children there is going to be the red sea because we have become a species divided against itself and thus cannot live in peace and cannot stand until this division is corrected.

Imhotep's mother was" a mortal named Kheredu-ankh, elevated later to semi-divine status by claims that she was the daughter of Banebdjedet." - [Marina Warner, Felipe Fernández-Armesto, World of Myths, University of Texas Press 2003, ISBN 0292702043, p.296

"Banebdjedet (Banedbdjed) was an Ancient Egyptian ram god with a cult centre at Mendes."

"Typically Banebdjedet was depicted with four rams heads to represent the four Ba's of the sun god.'- "Handbook of Egyptian mythology, Geraldine Pinch, p114-115, Oxford University Press, 2004

The four Ram heads relative to [Daniel 7:6 After this I beheld, and lo another, like a leopard, which had upon the back of it four wings of a fowl; the beast had also four heads; and dominion was given to it.]

[the beast had also four heads] = [Typically Banebdjedet was depicted with four rams heads]

So since you got the script as a child and you have not applied the remedy basically your God is a four headed Ram god. This indicates the scribes are certainly a cult of some fashion and their magic is script and math. These inventions are not wisdom education they are perhaps their ritual tools. So to put it in a sort of linear explanation. Imhotep's mother was the daughter of a deity known as Banebdjedet and this cult of this deity used script as a way to worship this deity and in using this script ritual one alters their perception permanently and mentally travels to this sense of time perception dimension and Imhotep was the key cult leader of this cult and he pushed the script and he was a spokesman for the script and made the script popular and made it so everyone would "eat of the script". This means there are only two factions on this planet. The ones that worship the four headed ram God Banebdjedet and they worship that God, the demotic God, by using the script ritual or tool and then there are the ones who deny the Ram God and apply the remedy after getting the script and they are what is known as worshipers of the True God, the unnamable God or the anti-script God or the anti-demotic God. Demotic of course is the name of the Egyptian script used by the common people. The complexity here is all the scripts in the world are descendents of this demotic script because all written languages are based on linear or sequential aspects, linear is a left brain trait. So this is all a nice way of saying if you are a human being and you got this as a child [3 R's: reading, writing and arithmetic -- the domain and strength of the left brain] you are a member of the Ram God cult and until you apply the remedy to return to normal perception dimension you are a worshiper of Banebdjedet and that is not good or bad that just is.

"It was the sexual connotations associated with his cult that led early Christians to demonise Banebdjedet."- "Handbook of Egyptian mythology, Geraldine Pinch, p114-115, Oxford University Press, 2004

The above comment is not exactly how it went but essentially the spirit of the comment is accurate. The Christians, Muslims and the Jews are the tribes and the tribes are the ones who applied the remedy to the demotic script and left the "ram god" cult. Perhaps an easier way to look at it is the ones in the ram god cult got the written education and they were mindfully in the alternate perception dimension and the ones who applied the remedy were mindfully in the normal perception dimension yet both were still living in the same physical dimension.

[John 7:43 So there was a division among the people because of him.] Denotes the battle between the scribes and the ones that understood there were problems with the script invention.

[Revelation 2:16 Repent; or else I will come unto thee quickly, and will fight against them(the scribes) with the sword of my mouth.]

[sword of my mouth.] = Oration as opposed to written language.

Demotic = commonly used hieroglyphics

In learning this invention: 3 R's: reading, writing and arithmetic -- the domain and strength of the left brain

It favors the left hemisphere and thus pushes one into an alternate perception dimension.

So it is like a drug that takes several years to administer and then it is permanent unless one applies the remedy or takes the antidote.

It is just like a hallucinogenic but it lasts a life time once applied or learned.

So Imhotep's mother was the daughter of Banebdjedet and Banebdjedet was a four headed ram god.

Imhotep was the patron saint of demotic script or of all scribes so he was like the cult leader that pushed or made script popular. Demotic means popular and in making it popular civilization started making other versions of it and everyone altered their perception and now civilization is a cult of scribes that are of this four headed ram god cult created by Imhotep. - 6:38:25 PM

7:05:49 PM - This demotic script was not known as characters, the characters were known as marks, and thus the comment the 'mark of the beast.'

What it comes down to is that modern society discriminates against the right hemisphere." - Roger Sperry (1973) Neurobiologist and Nobel Lauriat == Modern society is the cult of the ram god and veils the right hemisphere in all the children with their "mark" invention

A vain post on a forum:

I am going to explain this very simply. You are going to have to look into what I am suggesting and I am including the information for you.

[url]http://en.wikipedia.org/wiki/Imhotep[/url]

Imhotep is an Egyptian he is the patron saint of script. Other words he lived about 2600 BC and he perfected script, common hieroglyphics. The story goes his mother was the daughter of the four headed ram deity. His name means "One who comes in peace" relative to wolf in sheep's clothing, a being that looks like light but is in disguise. He was also a master architect and that requires math. Demotic is the word the Greeks used to describe the common everyday form Egyptian script. Demotic means popular. The problem is, the 3 R's: reading, writing and arithmetic -- the domain and strength of the left brain" So in learning this "popular" invention one veils their right hemisphere, the god image in man, the right hand side and in doing that alters a person's perception. A dimension is a level of consciousness.

What you perceive with right brain veiled after learning the written education is called the place of suffering or hell. So this popular invention pushes a person into the place of suffering because it alters their level of consciousness or their initial spirit. So this means any human being on the planet that got this reading, writing and arithmetic is a member of this ancient four headed ram cult and the only way to leave that cult is to apply the "deny one's self" remedy or also called "those that lose their life (mindfully) preserve it", preserve it means they return to normal spiritual or normal perception dimension and leave the cult of the four headed ram god started by Imhotep 2500 BC: So Imhoptep is the serpent in the garden :

[Genesis 3:1 Now the serpent was more subtil (charming)(imhoptep names means one who comes in peace) than any beast of the field which the LORD God had made. And he said unto the woman, Yea, hath God said, Ye shall not eat of every tree of the garden?

[Genesis 3:2 And the woman said unto the serpent(imhotep), We may eat of the fruit of the trees of the garden:

Genesis 2: 3 But of the fruit of the tree which is in the midst of the garden, God hath said, Ye shall not eat of it, neither shall ye touch it, lest ye die.

Genesis 3:4 And the serpent(Imhotep) said unto the woman, Ye shall not surely die(Imhotep said No its okay to learn my script and math , it makes you wise and popular(demotic means popular)

Genesis 3:5 For God doth know that in the day ye eat thereof, then your eyes shall be opened, and ye shall be as gods, (knowing good and evil.) = left brain traits is seeing parts or having prejudice.]

They did not call script characters, characters they called them marks. Thus the comment Marks of the beast, Imhotep(the one who comes in peace).

So Imhotpe was a commoner but he in a way reached a level of popularity with the Pharaoh or a level of power of the Pharaoh by being a master at written language and math so this was a way for a commoner to reach the "heights" of the Pharaoh or of the "gods" if they just learned this written language and math relative to selling your soul for wealth or popularity.

4/16/2010 6:13:48 PM – The scribes mock Judas and assume he was evil or bad but in reality he was just one of the beings that decided to attempt to apply the remedy Jesus suggested and so as he denied himself he went to the ninth circle of hell, treason and many do not survive that trip. So it is a miracle if a person firstly decides to apply the remedy because the only ones that are candidates are the meek or the depressed and out of them only a small fraction actually apply the remedy the full measure. The scribes make it seem like Judas killed Jesus but the truth is the scribes had no problem taking care of John the Baptist and taking care of all the disciples and so they would have taken care of Jesus one way or another. Judas was a concept that it is very important to go for the full measure application of the remedy because once one gets to the point of applying the remedy the ninth circle of hell, treason, must be confronted and that is a place one perhaps wishes to pass through swiftly.

[R. O. (16) committed suicide by hanging]

[A. M. (25) allegedly committed suicide by hanging]

These beings were in fact attempting to wake their self up but because right brain aspects where on a subconscious level the signals were crossed and they took the signals as literally defeat death as opposed to just mindfully defeat death and that is simply the way it goes once the right brain traits are veiled by the education. The emotional sensation of depression itself is the emotions ones experiences when right brain is coming to the surface and they are painful and harmful and often a being decides it is better to literally die but that is only because their cognitive ability is hindered and they are not aware those are simply symptoms right brain is unveiling. Certainly in the case of John the Baptist someone turned him in to the scribes also but that is a minor detail. The scribes are going to get who they need to get one way or another. The deeper reality is, if this remedy the many versions of it was just fiction or a joke or not true then there is no logical reason the scribes would need to harm any of those beings suggesting the remedy. Civilization itself can see the impact these beings that applied the remedy the full measure had on the entire structure of mankind. There is a certain fear the scribes have about this remedy because it works and it is truth and since it works and it is truth the remedy is the proof that the written education mentally hinders beings. Another way to look at it is, I accidentally applied the remedy and unveiled right brain well and with its vast processing power, pattern detection and intuition I was able to reverse engineer exactly what happened in a relatively short period of time. The only thing the scribes could be praying for at this moment in human history is that I am wrong about the remedy because once applied any human being will figure out in short order it factually was the written education that mentally hindered them and there certainly are restitutions the scribes must answer for above and beyond perhaps their ability to comprehend. We are talking about human beings conditioned mentally into a dangerously unsound state of mind on an industrial scale by human beings that were conditioned into a dangerously unsound state of mind on an industrial scale, and that is why all bets are off. Good luck burning my books because if the scribes cannot do that, it is all over for them. That's a nice way of saying the remedy works every time it is applied and if you doubt that apply it.

4/17/2010 12:21:45 AM –

[Genesis 1:1 In the beginning] Beginning of what? Time? Time relative to what? [Galatians 4:10 Ye observe days, and months, and times, and years.] = The scribes = the ones who have their right brain traits veiled so they have a strong sense of time because of all that left brain conditioning called the tree of knowledge, written education and math. And what is the goal of the ancient texts relative to suggesting the remedy to the neurosis caused by the tree of knowledge? [that there should be time no longer:]

[Revelation 10:6 And sware by him that liveth for ever and ever(infinity, no sense of time), who created heaven, and the things that therein are, and the earth, and the things that therein are, and the sea, and the things which are therein, [that there should be time no longer:]]

Simply put the tree of knowledge written language and math started this neurosis and thus began (time; the ones that sense time; the scribes) and one of the symptoms is one starts to have a strong sense of time and this is proof of the neurosis and so the goal of the remedy is to negate that neurosis so a being returns to sound mind or unveils right brain traits after the tree of knowledge veils them and then there will be time no longer relative to beings will no longer have the neurosis. It has a lot more to do with as a species accepting this tool we invented has some serious mental side effects and assisting everyone to escape that neurosis than an actual battle or war. It's enough of a battle to look at our own invention and submit it may have some bad side effects and doing that requires humility and vast amounts of it. Mankind's greatest invention, writing and math are also our greatest nightmare if not taught properly and that perhaps is the ultimate paradox relative to our species. The complexity is society as a whole has the neurosis so they have the right brain paradox aspect veiled so they only see written education and math as perfect and cannot look at it as a paradox at all. In the extreme left brain state one see's good and bad only, or parts, it is logical or expected. The mind cannot think in paradox if the paradox aspect of the mind is turned off is another way to look at it and the education turns that aspect off. If it is possible written education and math have unintended mental side effects then it is also potentially probable by seeing parts means one says "written education and math are either good or evil" relative to [Genesis 2:17 But of the tree of the knowledge of good and evil..]. This means the scribes/ the ones that sense time cannot see paradox they can only see good or evil but not good and evil at the exact same time. This neurosis or curse perpetuates itself because once a person gets enough of that education their entire perception is totally altered so they can only see a certain way and any attempts to see another way goes against their "goggles". One can only "see" what they perceive so the solution is not to make someone "see" something they cannot see the solution is to explain to them how to change their perception and then they can see properly and that is what the remedy does. I cannot force you to see holistically because if you sense time you can only see parts factually so the remedy realigns your perception then you see how you should see as if you never got the education in the first place. Of course the reality is to apply the remedy one has to deny their perception in a major way. Ones perception is going to say in a spooky place "something somehow is going to kill you", and then one has to say to their self "I do not care" and that is perhaps beyond the mental power of a person in the neurosis to accomplish certainly on a species level and so that means the curse caused by the education will be given to the next generation because the majority is unable to ever apply the remedy.

X = population six billion
Y = majority
Z = probable amount of beings that can apply the remedy

X * Z < Y = neurosis is unstoppable

Another way to look at it is if 100 people have the neurosis which means they got the education as children and 2 can apply the remedy then the majority is 8 that still has the neurosis and they will always vote to give the children the education and that perpetuates the neurosis. This means even if 49 out of 100 people apply the remedy the curse will still continue but that 45 number is very improbable even on a miracle standards because the remedy relies on each individual and the mental neurosis is very strong or likely permanent for the vast majority no matter what the incentives are. If the world announced , "every person that applies the remedy will get a billion dollars" the vast majority still could not apply the remedy simply because a symptom of the neurosis is the hypothalamus makes one very prone to fear and on top of that it hinders a beings reasoning ability or cognitive ability. The neurosis makes one afraid and unable to reason properly so they are trapped in that bubble. They may get to the point of understanding why they should apply the remedy but then they will be unable to apply the remedy because it requires great mental fortitude relative to the neurosis mental fortitude or a being may be willing to apply the remedy but then attempt to reason the need for doing it and talk their self out of applying the remedy. They will say "I am fine just the way I am" and that is logical because they never got a chance to feel their mind when it matures at the age of twenty because the education starts at six or seven. This is why in ancient texts they burned the cities of the scribes and this is why Jonah said "Should I not just kill all of the ones with the neurosis?". A scribe that has not mindfully died has no mindful life.

[Jonah 4:11 And should not I spare Nineveh, that great city, wherein are more than sixscore thousand persons that cannot discern between their right hand and their left hand; and also much cattle?]

It is an infinite loop that never ends because once a person has their complex right hemisphere veiled they are their own worst enemy. They are no longer mentally viable human beings until they apply the remedy. This also means on an individual level on can certainly attempt to apply the remedy and the good news is the ones in neurosis do not even believe the remedy works and do not believe the education has bad side effects and do not believe there is any validity to the remedy at all so one can apply it with no hindrance from the scribes because they are off in another perception dimension and are totally out of touch with reality on an absolute scale. The scribes have been turned from infinitely wise human beings into zombies in a matter of perhaps six or ten years starting at a very young age. At this stage I am so far adjusted to the no sense of time perception dimension I speak with the scribes and they are in a completely different perception reality all together. I am going away from them in perception. Every single day that passes I get further and further away from them relative to perception so I am unable to even make a single comment they do not see as insane or crazy or odd or weird. I woke up so well I have gone to the extreme of the no sense of time perception dimension in under two years relative to calendar.

[Exodus 13:12 That thou shalt set apart unto the LORD all that openeth the matrix, and every firstling that cometh of a beast which thou hast; the males shall be the LORD'S.]

This comment is suggesting all the males that apply the remedy shall be called Lords and in the east they are called Masters or Buddha but the terms are interchangeable so this entire concept of "the Lord" perhaps has not one single thing to do with supernatural at all. [the males shall be the LORD'S] This is logical because at this time, perhaps 4000 or 5000 years ago females did not get the written education so the only concern was when a male got the education they had to keep the covenant and apply the fear not remedy and then they were called the Lords. Now keeping that in mind look at this comment.

[Genesis 11:5 And the LORD came down to see the city and the tower, which the children of men builded.]

[And the LORD (a male that applied the remedy) came down(was spying on or keeping and eye on) to see the city(the city where the males , the scribes, were]

Now having said that I am certain if a being that has not applied the remedy and is very supernatural oriented because their cult leader who also did not apply the remedy said they should be supernatural oriented will see the above comments and say "That is not what it says." And this is why I have to write to myself because I am attempting to communicate with beings that are simply way too far mentally destroyed to even communicate with any longer. I am still not use to the fact I am unable to communicate with human beings that have been robbed of their cognitive ability. Once the education is pushed on them for even a few years their perception and right brain intuition starts to shift and then their cognitive ability is destroyed because it is relative to intuition and perception and attempting to bridge that reality is perhaps beyond anyone's ability.

Impossibility: something that cannot exist or cannot be done.

The only way you get better after you apply the remedy is to experiment because you will be in the machine state. So as you experiment with your testimony you ponder the results and get better at your testimony.

4/18/2010 12:18:00 AM – Now because you are in neurosis you have what you call self esteem issues. Firstly the only reason I can understand the ancient texts is because I unveiled right brain well and that means I have normal pattern detection and intuition and lightning fast random access processing abilities. It is logical since you are stuck with a Commodore 64 1 MHz processor mind I would appear wise with a 3.0K MHZ quad processor mind. I simply accidentally restored my right brain aspects after the written education veiled them and if you go into any other assumption direction than that you are mistaken.

[Exodus 13:12 That thou shalt set apart unto the LORD all that openeth the matrix, and every firstling that cometh of a beast which thou hast; the males shall be the LORD'S.

Exodus 13:13 And every firstling of an ass thou shalt redeem with a lamb(apply the remedy); and if thou wilt not redeem it, then thou shalt break his neck(any scribe that does not apply the remedy is a threat to the offspring): and all the firstborn of man among thy children shalt thou redeem.]

One way to look at it is I [openeth the matrix], but I am not a control freak so I suggest ways you can openeth the matrix also.

Matrix : a substance in which something is embedded or enclosed.

[embedded or enclosed] Is relative to the scribes are closed minded and this is only because their right brain aspects have been veiled by the education.

[Your account has been locked for the following reason: Agenda of contempt for Christianity & Catholiciasm. This change will be lifted: Never]

It is logical that since I have applied the remedy and have returned to normal perception dimension I should be looked at as reverse to the ones still in the alternate perception dimension. I should appear "bad" relative to the scribes with closed minds because now I have an open mind. That is logical and an expected result. This is a symptom of rift or division because of the reality of the two alternate perception dimensions. So relative to the above comment in suggesting the written education is the tree of knowledge I am in contempt of the scribes agenda because if I am not in contempt of their agenda they are in contempt. The scribes have very strong ego's and pride as a result of having their mind bent to the left by the education so it is logical they would have difficultly facing their self. For example:

[Matthew 7:29 For he taught them as one having authority, and not as the scribes.]

This is saying Jesus was using a logic that was unlike the scribes, not some of the scribes all of the scribes. So then one has to ask what is a scribe? Any human being on the planet that got that written education and math and did not apply the remedy to restore their right brain traits, the god image in man. So in suggesting that comment I am judging all human beings that got the written education because they are known as scribes but scribes have this huge pride so they cannot face that reality but sometimes the meek scribes which are the depressed or suicidal scribes can relate to what I am saying because depression is a symptom the right brain traits are attempting to unveil. So because I have cognitive ability I can understand why this would happen:

[Your account has been locked for the following reason: Agenda of contempt for Christianity & Catholiciasm. This change will be lifted: Never]

I am fully aware it is logical beings who have not applied the remedy would mock me simply because I am communicating to them from proper perception dimension and everything I say in many respects is contrary to what they perceive in alternate perception dimension. The deeper reality is the scribes are hesitant to grasp what I suggest because what I suggest means they are completely wrong and have to deny their self to the absolute degree and start all over and a being with these symptoms of pride and ego are not willing to do that or face that reality. The majority is never going to allow a minority to attack their principles willingly. So when dealing with the scribes the "truth" will always harm them. What is the truth? The tree of knowledge is written education, reading and math. That harms the scribes because that is their golden calf and their God. So by suggesting said truth on their forum I am attacking their God and they will do anything in their power to stop that.

[Matthew 23:25 Woe unto you, scribes and Pharisees, hypocrites! for ye make clean the outside of the cup and of the platter, but within they are full of extortion and excess.]

This is a repeat comment in spirit to this comment:

[Luke 20:46 Beware of the scribes, which desire to walk in long robes, and love greetings in the markets, and the highest seats in the synagogues, and the chief rooms at feasts;]

[which desire to walk in long robes] = [for ye make clean the outside of the cup and of the platter]

And is also a repeat in spirit of this comment:

[Matthew 7:15 Beware of false prophets(scribes), which come to you in sheep's clothing, but inwardly they are ravening wolves.]

[which come to you in sheep's clothing] = [which desire to walk in long robes] = [for ye make clean the outside of the cup and of the platter]

[but within they are full of extortion and excess] = [but inwardly they are ravening wolves.]

Why are they ravening wolves inwardly? Because they got the written education and it veiled their right hemisphere and so they are mentally unsound and thus are not acting like human beings of sound mind act so they are beasts or lunatics and act as such. Only an insane person would mentally harm a child by pushing all the left brain favoring education on them and not even be aware of it at all. Only an insane person would mentally harm a child and then not tell the child the remedy to that mental harm or perhaps that is the definition of the sinister. That's a nice way to say to every single scribe in this narrow, I eat for no reason so bring everything you have when you come. I am not making a last stand against the scribes I am probing their defenses and looking for patterns of weakness to exploit. I would never write that in my books only in my personal diaries. On one hand that it is perhaps very dangerous explaining to the scribes what the tree of knowledge really is but on the other hand they mostly just mock it and suggest I am insane so it is not dangerous at all perhaps. The scribes would say I am less insane if I said the tree of knowledge was an alien spaceship or a lizard man than if I say it is written language and math. By suggesting the tree of knowledge is written language and math the scribes are faced with what they perceive is impossibility and also a plate of crow far beyond their ability to swallow so their only logical response is to assume I must be insane because if I am not they factually are. The scribes are perhaps far more comfortable with ghosts than reality. Relative to my perception I am just saying if you get all that left brain favoring education as a child you must then perform this one second mental exercise remedy to negate all the left brain favoring education mental side effects and that is perhaps way beyond the scribe's ability to grasp. This is an indication that the cognitive ability in the scribes is greatly hindered by the education. Simple cause and effect relationships become this huge mountain they cannot climb or even perhaps consider climbing. The education has turned the scribes from infinitely wise beings into mentally sad beasts of burden. My purpose is to make the word scribe the worst of all profanities.

Profanity : language or behavior that shows disrespect for God, any deity, or religion.

[written language when taught improperly and when the remedy is not applied afterwards shows disrespect for God by discriminating against the right hemisphere the God image in man.]

[Luke 20:46 Beware of the scribes..]

I am leaning on the side of the fence that suggests we are so intelligent we invented written language and math and in learning these inventions they favored left brain so much it veiled right brain aspects and that made us mentally unsound and since we are mentally unsound we are out of harmony and so we are a self harmer species so since we are self harmer species as a result of this education induced neurosis the solution is to encourage mental self harm which is what denying one's self is. The complexity in that is everyone in the neurosis has different things they fear. Some are more afraid of words than others. Some are more afraid of certain music than others. This fear is really aversion and is a symptom of the neurosis. So it appears to the scribes this denying oneself is breaking the rules and so they dislike that because it seems dangerous and because they are afraid of bad haircuts it must be encouraged with the understanding the vast majority of the scribes are fatalities to the neurosis and will never ever be able to escape the neurosis caused by the written education. This requires a being that has applied to the remedy to be indifferent because if the being attempts to show emotions in this situation they never will be able to suggest these things because their tendency is to be in harmony so they must deny that nature and achieve disharmony. This is where the risk comes in and this is why the ancient texts were underground, secret, occult or hidden. This secretive aspect creates a lot of problems because the point is to make the understanding that written education and math has unwanted mental side effects a common well known fact everyone knows and understands. For example no one is ashamed asbestoses can cause lung cancer it is just a well known fact. So attempting to mask what the tree of knowledge literally is will only confuse the scribes, the ones in neurosis even further. This situation does not require a person to appear holier than thou because all that does is make's the ones in neurosis even more confused. This whole aspect of "I am better than you" in "religion" is total stupidity. Firstly any being in any of the big religions that does not know exactly what the tree of knowledge relates to literally should be considered nothing but a novice and should be looked at as such. The ones that apply the remedy are the Lords but not in a "I am better than you" aspect but simply they are human beings that understand the tree of knowledge and understand the remedy but that is as far as it goes and that means their only purpose is to make other human beings Lords also. The core problem is unless the written education is not seen as having potentially unwanted side effects then the children are going to be conditioned into the neurosis and so that is the bottom line effort. Unless the leak in the boat is stopped the boat will sink. The potential for bloodshed and war is massive but we are a self harming species in this neurosis so that is logical. Simply put we are killing ourselves with the education anyway and we have such strong prejudice in this seeing part's left brain state which is all a part of the neurosis. We are prone to harm ourselves and each other no matter what we do because as a species we are in neurosis so the risk in attempting to solve this problem is great but that is irrelevant because if the problem is not resolved we remain self harmers anyway. We are killing the offspring by mentally hindering them so to suggest war or bloodshed is so bad is stupidity. We are mentally killing the offspring so everything after that is meaningless. A species cannot be more of a self harmer than when it is systematically mentally killing the offspring and is not even aware of it. The scribes see literal death is worse than mentally destroying the offspring but in fact they are the same exact thing. The scribes will suggest these stupid suicide rates for students in school and say "Seven out of 100,000 student kill their self." And assume that is some wise statistic but the truth is any human that kills their self because of depression or because of tragedy like a stress situation does that because the education veiled their right brain random access thought process aspect's and that applies for the persons entire life if they do not apply the remedy; if a person becomes depressed at thirty and kills their self that is because of the school education. If a person kills their self because of depression at the age of fifty that is a school related suicide. If a person becomes addicted to drugs and eventually dies from that it is because of the education. The scribes can only see one step in front of their nose and so they see half truths and half pictures but perhaps never the whole picture. The scribes are concerned about the economy and money and at the exact same time are mentally destroying all the offspring and have no idea they are doing that so they have absolutely no cognitive ability relative to priorities. They are killing the offspring with the education and then are concerned about stupidity and so since they are blind to the damage the education causes they are blind to the remedy to the neurosis caused by the education. Unless the scribes first understand the education causes mental problems then they will never be able to understand the remedy so their money and economy is nothing but stupidity. So the scribes have to have this tree of knowledge information crammed down their throats until they choke on it or wake up to it. This will certainly create a division in the species and that is logical but as it is now the scribes are making it look like the beings that speak out against the methods of the education are evil but in reality the scribes are the ones mentally hindering the children so they are to be looked at as abominations because only an abomination would harm a child in any way. The scribes are totally insane so they cry over split milk so once that is understood one just tells them how it is and if they speak mockingly tell them to shut up and at least that will give them some emotions to block. The scribes will say "Don't speak angry at me" and then they will turn around and go mentally kill the children and not even believe they are so they are to be treated verbally relative to what they are, mentally conditioned unsound human beings. Until they apply the remedy what they say does not matter at all, they are insane. Now this means they may kill you for speaking out against the tree of knowledge but they may not because they only see a person that has applied the remedy as crazy or insane. Insanity see's sanity as insanity. The deepest reality is the scribes are factually mentally hindering children with all their left brain favoring education and they factually do not believe they are so they factually know not what they do and that is the definition of an insane person. The point is the ones in neurosis, the scribes have 10% of their mind working and so they do not believe they have infinitely powerful minds so one has to test their mind or put their mind to the test. The scribes are afraid of words and pictures and colors and music so they are what you would call fickle or changeable, easy to manipulate. The scribes are like dragsters with huge engines but they only have one spark plug working so they forgot they are dragsters so to encourage them will only enforce their belief they are not dragsters. To enforce the belief that human beings are afraid or ashamed of words, pictures, sounds or music is stupidity. Schools paddle children that cuss and they get the permission of the governments and the parents. My patience is running thin. If you have a poison mushroom patch call me because I am infinitely hungry.

4/18/2010 3:48:46 PM - "Little minds have little worries, big minds have no time for worries." - Emerson

This comment by Emerson is a good example of comments having unseen meanings. All it is really saying is "little minds" are minds that have not applied the remedy and thus they sense time mindfully and "big minds" have no sense of time because they have right brain unveiled and the paradox aspect factors into their perception of time; "Time has passed and no time has passed"; and they have no worries because they are in the machine state or in the now. Worry is a sense of time symptom like greed, lust, stress etc.

[Little minds] = ones in neurosis, right brain veiled.

[little worries] = ignorant, vain concerns.

[big minds] = sound minds

[have no time] = no sense of time

[for worries] = Contempt for the ones with little worries, the little minds, the scribes.

So the ones that have applied the remedy are mocking the scribes using "wise quotes" and only the ones who have applied the remedy get the jokes. Some of the "wise quotes" are inside jokes from sound minded human beings mocking the mentally unsound human beings, the scribes. Of course this tradition was started in the ancient texts. So it is like a secret society that does not want to be secret but the scribes have their minds veiled and hindered so they just simply cannot get the jokes.

I assure you this is a jab at the scribes, the ones that sense time but even saying that you still may not believe it.

"Little minds have little worries, big minds have no time for worries." - Emerson

Of course in the left brain extreme state one tends to seek absolutes and the reverse of absolutes is probability and that is because of the ambiguity aspect of right brain. So one can also see this comment like this:

[Little minds] = ones in neurosis, right brain veiled.

[little worries] = ignorant , vain concerns.

[big minds] = sound minds

[have no time] = no sense of time

[for worries] = To busy attempting to wake up the species from the neurosis caused by the tree of knowledge.

Once you apply the remedy the full measure all you do is talk about the remedy, talk about the ones in neurosis, talk about methods and strategies to reach the ones in neurosis. This is an indication that as long as we are a species in neurosis we will continue to put the children into neurosis and until that stops, absolutely nothing matters at all. If you think anything else in the universe matters besides attempting to stop the species from putting everyone in neurosis with the education you are infinitely ignorant and blind as a bat. You may think all your little concerns matter but they do not matter at all in contrast to this neurosis loop we are in, you are just too mentally destroyed to grasp that perhaps. We are a species that mentally kills all the offspring and you perceive you are able to convince me anything other than addressing that matters at all? Perhaps your entire life revolves around this: [little worries] and perhaps you hang around to many beings with this: [Little minds]. Perhaps all those little scribe minds you hang around with have convinced you your little worries are of value. Perhaps it is best you stay out of my sea.

Everyone is born with = [big minds]
Then the education turns their mind into = [Little minds]
Then one applies the remedy and returns to = [big minds]

The complexity is very few return to big minds and the stupidity is there are forms of education such as oral education that would never turn the mind into a little mind, but of course we are living in an insane asylum so reason and sanity are not very prevalent here except in closed circles.

4/19/2010 10:17:56 PM –

This is a translation of the story of the Pied Piper in the Lueneburg manuscript (c. 1440–50) as suggested by www.triune.de

"In the year of 1284, on the day of Saints John and Paul on 26 June
130 children born in Hamelin were seduced
By a piper, dressed in all kinds of colours,
and lost at the place of execution near the koppen."

This is simply a parable. The scribes are the pied piper. The music represents charming the children and the multicolored clothes represent materialism. The suggestion of Saints John and Paul suggest the scribes harm the children right in front of the beings that have applied the remedy and they are powerless to stop it. So for example the scribes say 'People who are well educated are smarter and live better lives" or "People who are well educated make more money and have more luxury." So the music the pied piper (the scribes) plays is the propaganda and the clothes are the potential rewards for getting the education. The children are new to the world so they see this piper, the scribes', and the scribes are just like a child molester who is saying "If you get in my car (get the written education) I will give you some candy(material wealth)." This appears like a conspiracy but in reality the scribes in that state of mind know not what they do so they do things they perceive are wise but in reality they are unwise. This is the equation.

X = mentally unsound lunatic
Y = deduction
Z = result

X + Y = Z

(Z) is always going to be a nightmare because a lunatic is unable to make proper cognitive decisions. A scribe will proclaim to the universe "If we start the education on the child when they are six they will certainly become wise." but in reality they are factually meaning to say "I was harmed starting at six and I want to make sure all the children are harmed like I was starting at the age of six so they will be like I am." and this is relative to misery loves company. The scribers were abused mentally to such a degree they are only capable of abuse relative to inflicting it on their self and others not as much verbally as literally. For example telling a child they are bad is not literal abuse but forcing a child by law to undergo years of left brain favoring education to the point it completely alters that child's mind and thus that child's perception and leaves that child with 10% mental capability is literal abuse. The scale the scribes were abused as children is on a level they do not even want the children they mentally abuse or put in the neurosis to recover either. The deepest reality is the scribes are factually infinitely wise beings that have been mentally hindered and are doing things they are not even aware of at all. The scribes are suffering so greatly their suffering is being taken out on completely innocent children but they do not perceive that is what is happening. This "anger" or "rage" they are exhibiting by their deeds, relative to pushing all the education on children, is what this river of Styx, river of anger, aspect is all about once one applies the remedy. One can look at it like, after they apply the remedy they restore their mind and become aware of how abused they were and they go through quite a long period of anger and rage cerebrally and that is logical and that is what any person that is abused tends to go through but the scale relative to this mental abused caused by the education is far beyond any anger one can compare to. Here is an example of the anger after one applies the remedy:

[Exodus 2:11 And it came to pass in those days, when Moses was grown(applied the remedy), that he went out unto his brethren, and looked on their burdens(how the ones with no sense of time were being taken advantage of by the scribes): and he spied an Egyptian smiting an Hebrew(one who had applied the remedy or a tribe member that never got the education), one of his brethren.

Exodus 2:12 And he looked this way and that way, and when he saw that there was no man(no scribe), he slew the Egyptian(scribe), and hid him in the sand.]

The right brain intuition is so strong one is just aware they got mentally raped on a scale so great they can never get justice for it ever and they are ripped apart by that because they have this thought that "Who would do this to me as a child and what did I do?" but on a scale that is so great one is simply pure rage for perhaps the first several months after they apply the remedy and right brain unveils. The anguish so to speak is firstly because one realizes they got abused and then they realize the children are having the same thing done to them and there is no way to stop it or even do anything about it and then the grief is multiplied and so a being has to simply block all those emotions completely because they are emotions that are proper emotions relative to the abuse but in this narrow there is no such thing as justice at all. One seeks justice in a place there is no justice yet one naturally wants justice and they can never get justice ever. The scribes are factually infinitely wise beings that have their minds turned down to 10% and that makes them so angry they want maximum abuse potential and the children offer them that. Another way to look at it is the only thing that is keeping the scribes from being infinitely wise is the remedy and once they apply that they no longer exhibit this rage or abusive nature because they wake up and are aware that is what they were doing. So this whole "war" that has been going on for thousands of years is simply beings that woke up from the neurosis and saw what they were doing in that neurosis attempting to wake up the scribes so the scribes can see what they are doing relative to abusing children. The abused(scribes) become abusive(on the children) via the written education. Sometimes you will hear a person addicted to drugs giving their own child the drugs and that is what is can be compared to. A person on the drugs is miserable and so they want to make sure their child is miserable would be the concept. It is logical the scribes would deny that because they are still in the abuse stage. The scribes have grown to love to abuse the children because it makes them feel like they are not the only ones that were abused. This is all happening subconsciously in their mind. The scribes are subconsciously fully aware they are harming children but those signals are so silenced they never reach the conscious state of mind and this is perhaps a natural blocking method to protect them in their strong emotional state. One way to look at it is , if you were going about your life thinking you were doing good at life and someone came up to you and said "Why are you killing all the children and we can prove it and show you that you are killing children even though you have been thinking you are doing good?", the being may have a complete emotional collapse. It is like a serial killer who will always tell himself killing is righteous because if he ever realized killing was horrible he could perhaps not bear what he has done. The waking up process is so difficult because it is like running a marathon and in the last few feet of the race a person comes up to you and says "The race starts tomorrow and everything you have accomplished today means nothing." "You just ran a marathon but it does not count at all." This is all relative to this meek state of mind one has to be in to apply the remedy. One has to be in a state of mind to be open to the reality everything they thought was their life was really a symptom they were mentally dead. Nothing carries over after the remedy is applied. For example a person may have donated lots of money to education and then they apply the remedy and realize they did a huge amount of damage by doing that but at the time they perceived they were doing much good. One may have been a teacher in school and thought " I am good for teaching the children for 20 years" and then apply the remedy and realize they perhaps could have not done more harm and damage to children even if they tried as hard as they could consciously. One may be a principle in school and then apply the remedy and then realize they were just an overseer of the abuse of children on a scale they may never recover from. This is all relative to the alternate perception realities. What applies in one perception reality is the reverse on an absolute scale in the other perception reality relative to the reverse thing.

Compulsory Education Law = It is required to abuse all the children mentally or one is deemed a criminal and a threat to children. The scribes do not see it that way because they seek maximum abuse to make up for the abuse they sustained but they are only aware of that on a subconscious level.

A scribe parent has to abuse children so they can function and withstand the amount of abuse they suffered from the education on a mental level. Human beings can only take so much mental hindering before they snap and just start harming the children on an industrial scale and that is what modern society really is. Human beings that have snapped mentally from all the mental hindering caused to them in their "education years" and they are just mentally ripping the children to shreds and they consciously factually do not even think they are doing that. The only way to get out of insanity is to do things you think are insane because that is the only way to break the cycle of insanity.

[1 Corinthians 3:20 And again, The Lord(the ones that applied the remedy the Lords) knoweth the thoughts of the wise(the scribes), that they are vain.]

Buddha called the scribes the sane and the ancient texts call the scribes the wise; quite comedic. This is a symptom of the alternate perception reality, they are completely contrary. After all that left brain education you are wise as long as your definition of wise is foolish or stupid and you are sane as long as your definition of sane is completely insane. The only possible way ever an insane person can become sane again is to do things they perceive are insane and that is exactly what deny yourself means. If you perceive some music is evil or bad or foolish to listen to you better buy that music and listen to it until you become indifferent to it. If you think a word is evil or bad you better say that word until you are indifferent to it. If you think a picture of a dead body is evil or bad you better look at it until you are indifferent to it. That is what deny yourself is. Your stupidity laws do not really apply you just are infinitely delusional and think they do. I don't listen to what insane people say I better do. You may perceive the ones that are awake care about living but the truth is this existence is not living any longer it is just a lunatic asylum full of lunatics that love to mentally abuse innocent children and they do it openly and brag about it and even have laws that say everyone has to abuse the children or they are criminal. You would be wise to never say the words justice , civility, lawfulness, compassion or mercy around me because I will simply attempt to convince you to go mindfully kill yourself as a natural reaction to keep from throwing up on you. - 11:23:12 PM

4/20/2010 12:59:16 AM – This is relative to world war 2. What were the base symptoms relative to psychology for world war 2 relative to the main axis powers?

Greed for land. Lust for control. Arrogance or pride known as nationalism. Envy that other countries had more land. Greed for resources. Envy that other countries had resources the main axis powers did not have. In seeking these greed's or lusts or to satisfy these envy aspects wrath was employed which was the literal physical war. The main goal in seeking these greed's and lusts was to achieve a state of extravagance which is gluttony. For example the axis powers wanted to take over the world and take over everything as in the resources and wealth and also control everyone they conquered. So all of these psychological aspects are relative to the extreme left brain state the education puts one in. It makes a person able to maintain these mental symptoms like greed, envy, pride, wrath, lust gluttony because the right brain random access thoughts no longer figure into the thought processes. One cannot be a control freak if they mentally cannot maintain a state of wanting to control and that applies to greed, envy, lust and gluttony as well. It is similar to sometimes a person wants something very bad but after a while they forget about it and then after a while they forget they even wanted that object or thing except when right brain is unveiled this is on a minute basis and not a year or month basis relative to a calendar. Another way to look at it is right brain random access processing is so fast one can come up with an idea and reach the final conclusion of that idea and determine it is not a well thought out idea in about one minute relative to a clock. Now in contrast to world war 2 the axis powers started a war and it took them years to conclude that was not a well thought out idea. World War 2 was factually just another symptom of how human beings behave when they have their mind bent to the left as children as a result of having all that left brain favoring education pushed on them at such a young age. Your cult leader and your government leader and your "experts" will never come to that conclusion because that conclusion requires sound minded logic and complexity to reach but the beings in the ancient texts told our species things like world war 2 would happen if we did not apply the remedy after eating off the tree of knowledge.

[Genesis 2:17 But of the tree of the knowledge(reading writing and math) of good and evil(favors left brain and makes one start to see parts), thou shalt not eat of it: for in the day that thou eatest thereof thou shalt surely die.]

This line is simply saying, if you get all that left brain reading, writing and math and do not apply the remedy you will see many parts, have many aversions, probably start to hate certain kinds of people, be envious of them, lust for what they have and you do not have,

109

and you will become wrathful and want to take that stuff from them and perhaps even kill them to take that stuff you envy from them and you will die and they will die in the process. To explain it in a simple way so you may possibly be able to grasp it, human beings cannot exist properly with their right brain aspects veiled even slightly let alone completely. So many tens of thousands of human being died in world war 2 alone because of the tree of knowledge and because as a species we never questioned those inventions and we never understood the importance of the remedy after teaching those inventions and every leader in this world right now does not have the mental ability to grasp, understand or believe that. You are just a little mouse and I am a giant cat and no matter what you say about me at the end of the day I am going to swat you around like a little toy because I don't know what else to do with you. Every 24 hour period relative to a clock that passes I become more aware and you stay right where you are in the dust. I am in a machine state and every time I hear something or read something I punch that information into the machine and come out with further understandings and become more aware. That cycle is happening so fast I simply do not even write down all the things I come to new understandings about anymore because my hands do not type fast enough to keep up. My mouth cannot talk fast enough to keep up with the amount of understandings I am coming to on a minute by minute basis. This is how powerful right brain is when it is in full working order and this is why Abraham and Lot killed every single scribe in the two cities because they knew the scribes were destroying unnamable power. Abraham and Lot knew those scribes were destroying God. Abraham and Lot killed the scribes because the scribes were killing the God image in man. In perhaps a billion years the scribes still will not be able to figure out what the tree of knowledge is. In order for the scribes to understand what the tree of knowledge is they have to look at their self in a judgmental state of mind and find fault with their golden calf wisdom invention and their pride and ego will never allow that. It is logical mankind has developed machines and it is logical mankind can make robots that cover the logic aspects well but they have trouble emulating emotions because emotions on the scale that scribes have are abnormal and thus difficult to emulate. The straightforward logic is it is easy to create an emotionless robot and that is because that is naturally how human beings are in the sound mind state. The strong emotional capacity is abnormal in human beings and is a symptom the education has made the mind unsound and that is why they are hard to create in robots. The pharmaceutical companies are making trillions of dollars off of treating all these emotional symptoms caused by all the left brain favoring education. This is an indication of the insanity our species is in because we are factually creating the emotional problems and then attempting to treat them and at the exact same time have no idea what is causing them and so we are creating more emotional problems in the next generation via the written education. Insanity is the inability to detect what is causing one to act the way they do.

4/20/2010 6:02:43 AM -

X = boat
Y = leak
Z = bailing water from boat
A = creating more leaks in boat

X + Y = Z

So we identify there is a problem relative to emotional aspects but we never identify what causes them so we continue to create more so we are in a perpetual suffering.

(Z < A) is the suffering. We cannot bail the water out of the boat as fast as we are pouring water back into the boat so we are self defeating. The boat will sink because we are creating more leaks than we can bail out and this is not on a country scale this is on a species scale. If you observe the suicide rate of children in written education schools you will see it is uniform all across the globe which means it is not just a symptom that suicide in children is just normal it is a symptom the written education is detrimental no matter what written language is taught. Depression is uniform in the species it just comes out as different things. Some countries have great drug problems. Some countries have lots of mental illness. Some countries have lots of crime aspects but these are all symptoms of depression, economic depression, psychological depression; human beings that are suffering. The story of Job is the taste test so to speak. Take any scribe on the planet and take away their house, their money, their friends, their family and their health and see how they react. In the machine state one can only focus on the now, so all of those attachments do not really have much of an impact on one psychology, or on the mindset of a person. This has a lot to do with standards or pride in the scribe state of mind. Some scribes would rather kill their self than be fat or have no money or have no place to live or have no friends or have an illness. In the machine state one continues until one is unable to continue. There is no emotional attachment to death or loss. You see stories on the news and say there is a shooting and a person is being interviewed and they say "It was horrible and I am afraid and scared and frightened." That is a symptom they are very afraid of even the possibility of loss and what that means is they may do some very strange things to avoid loss or the perception of loss, the perception of loss of self pride or self esteem or self worth. It is ironic perhaps that the scribes will say take pride in your work and at the same time they will say pride is one of the seven deadly sins. Pride is really a symptom the ego is turned up way to high.

[S. W. (31) is accused of choking his wife T. W. (28) to death with a belt one day before their divorce was to be final]

111

This has to do with pride and inability to tolerate loss. In a life system there is great potential for loss so if one has an aversion to loss they are doomed to suffer. "I lost my keys." , "I lost my hair.", "I lost some weight." ,"I lost my best friend.", "I lost the bet.", "I lost my relative.", "We lost the war.", "I am at a loss for words.", "I lost my wife to a divorce so now no one is going to get her."

[S. W. (31) is accused of choking his wife T. W. (28) to death with a belt one day before their divorce was to be final.]

The problem with the language is the words are absolutes and they can frustrate a being that is mentally unsound like a scribe.

[J.S. (49) committed suicide by ligature strangulation after losing his job.]

Losing his job; the beings in the Amazon have absolutely no luxuries in contrast to an average being in society and they do not kill their self. Perception is everything and so if one perceives they "lost" they may very well determine that is more than they can bare. Perception is relative to cognitive ability and cognitive ability is relative to the frontal lobe and the frontal lobe does not develop until a human being is past their 20's and perhaps 25 and by that time they have perhaps 12 years of left brain favoring education under their belt because education starts at six or seven. You may blame the man who strangled his wife and blame the man who killed himself after losing his job but first you have to blame yourself for not questioning the education methods. If I give you a hit of acid and you go out and kill people or yourself it is my fault. If I give you a hit of acid and you go out and destroy the entire planets eco system it is my fault. Before you lock anyone in jail you better look at what you do first and what you support first and that little compulsory education law first. I am mindful the scribes will continue to mentally harm the children because they are no longer mentally viable as beings. I am mindful in two hours the children will be forced to go to school and no one will explain to them the potential side effects of all that education and will not suggest to them the remedy to the unwanted mental side effects. You can dream I have morals but your dreams will only end up as nightmares.

4/20/2010 7:52:24 PM - Disorder of Written Expression - A disorder resulting from problems in poor writing skills.

This "disorder" is exactly what this comment is referring to.
"What it comes down to is that modern society discriminates against the right hemisphere."
- Roger Sperry (1973) Neurobiologist and Nobel Lauriat

Simply put some extreme left brain being has determined if a human being cannot use the left brain favoring manmade writing invention well they certainly must have mental problems. Here are some associated features in this disorder.

Low Self-Esteem
Social problems
Increased Dropout rate at School

I imagine if I had scribes telling me I have a mental disorder because I can't use their left brain favoring written language well, use all the commas well, use "proper" sequential sentence structure well, I would perhaps have low self esteem, social problems and also be looking for a way to drop out of school.

These are some aspects that may be related or may need to be ruled out before one of the wise psychologists scribes can be certain the person has this "disorder" of written expression.

Conduct Disorder
Attention Deficit Disorder
Depression
Other Learning Disorders

Conduct disorder. If you cannot follow all the education rules and write like everyone else does you certainly have conduct disorders. It's all just control based fear tactics using elementary pinprick logical to come to conclusions which are not based on anything but stupidity. "If you don't spell the word cat like we told you to, you are a trouble maker and have conduct disorder."

Attention Deficit Disorder; I will cover this one swiftly. Perhaps the child does not like to listen to mental abomination retard idiot scribes so they ignore you and you hate that so you determine it is their fault because in your delusional conditioned state of mind you would not know wisdom if it was writing infinite books to you.

Depression: This is an interesting one because when a person is depressed it is a symptom their right brain is attempting to unveil itself and so it is logical their left brain writing skills would begin to suffer. As depression increases it is logical writing ability which is left brain focused would decrease.

Other Learning Disorders: Keep in mind Einstein dropped out of school or was kicked out of school at 16 and he suggested math hindered his creativity and creativity is a right brain trait so he would be classified as having a learning disorder. I did okay in school but I was very shy and depressed and had lots of emotional problems even by the age of 15. I am certain many children have those problems also but they tend to keep them to their self because they don't want the lunatic scribes to catch wind of it because the lunatic scribes will just throw lots of pills at them and explain how many disorders they have and that makes the child feel even worse. The beings that appear to be doing just fine and have no outward emotional problems are the most screwed up of all because they are so mentally destroyed by the education they are afraid to show any weakness and the ones that openly suggest they are depressed are at least open minded enough to detect something is wrong. You do not have to explain to me how all the education did not hinder your mind to a great degree because I already know it factually did and your fruits prove it.

[S. H. (16) brought a gun to school and shot himself because of bad grades.]

Beware of the scribes little ones.

Dyscalculia: Dyscalculia basically means difficulty performing mathematical calculations, specifically; it means a learning disability which affects math. Like dyslexia, dyscalculia can be caused by a visual perceptual deficit and also along with dyslexia, its effects varies tremendously in each individual.

When right brain is at full power it is the dominate aspect in the mind because right hemisphere aspects are more powerful than left hemisphere aspects. At 50/50 mental harmony one see's holistically and does not see things so much in parts. This means when dealing with math which is all parts based, absolutes, one has problems coping math because right brain only see's zero or infinity well, the extremes, and math requires one to only see tiny parts which denotes judgment. So it is perfectly logical a person of sound mind would have issues doing math and because this disorder is suggested along the lines of dyslexia which is simply a symptom the right brain random access aspects are figuring greatly into the persons thought processes it is clear to see this is nothing but discrimination against right hemisphere.

This is the strategy to cure a child of this "disorder". Following identification, parents and teachers should work together to establish strategies that will help the student learn mathematics more effectively.

That comment is saying: Following identification the left brain influenced scribe parents and the left brain influenced scribe teachers should work together to establish strategies that will help that innocent child fully veil their right hemisphere traits more effectively.

Dyslexia: Developmental Reading Disorder (DRD) or Dyslexia is defect of the brains higher cortical processing of symbols. Children with DRD may have trouble rhyming and separating the sounds in spoken words. As measured by standardized tests, the patient's ability to read (accuracy or comprehension) is substantially less than you would expect considering age, intelligence and education. This deficiency materially impedes academic achievement or daily living.

This entire "disorder" is nothing but a human being showing a great degree of right brain characteristics.

[As measured by a standardized tests] = Left brain favoring tests and anyone who cannot pass these left brain favoring tests are deemed mentally unsound which means any being that has even slight right brain traits is deemed mentally unsound and thus the comment: "What it comes down to is that modern society discriminates against the right hemisphere."
- Roger Sperry (1973) Neurobiologist and Nobel Lauriat

[This deficiency materially impedes academic achievement or daily living.] What this comment means is if you cannot pass all the left brain tests and left brain favoring standard tests you will end up with a slave job and you will be nothing but an outcast in the cult of the four headed ram.

Modern society is simply extreme left brain conditioned beings and they do not tolerate any child or being that is not extreme left brain like they are and when they see one they either deem them mentally unsound or they discriminate against them,

The solution to these "disorders" is always push more left brain favoring education on them. Hire teachers and tutors and get the parents involved and just push these left brain favoring inventions on the children from all angles. Use fear tactics and punishment and make the child veil their right hemisphere so they can be cured of their Conduct Disorder.

[Job 18:3 Wherefore are we counted as beasts, and reputed vile in your sight?]

Modern society is counted as vile beasts in my sight.
Reputed: widely believed, although not necessarily established as fact.
Vile: extremely unpleasant to experience; causing disgust or abhorrence; of little or no worth.
Abhorrence: somebody or something that is strongly disapproved of.

The greatest accomplishment the scribes will ever achieve is when they mindfully kill their self. I submit I am either the most evil being in this narrow or I am the only being in this narrow telling the truth without any sugar coating.

4/21/2010 8:49:32 AM - Dysthymic Disorder: Dysthymic Disorder is characterized by chronic depression, but with less severity than a major depression. The essential symptom for dysthymic disorder is an almost daily depressed mood for at least two years, but without the necessary criteria for a major depression. Low energy, sleep or appetite disturbances and low self-esteem are usually part of the clinical picture as well.

This "disorder" is simply a human being with their right brain traits veiled and they are on the edge of being suicidal outwardly but inwardly they are in full blown suicidal mode and that means they are in the end stages of right brain unveiling. The rule of thumb is they are in this mild form of depression for so long relative to a calendar because with right brain veiled their thought processes are very slothful. Their actual depression started long before they reached this stage of appearing depressed to those around them. So this type of person will either go into major depression and major suicidal thoughts or they will stay at this stage of mild depression for the rest of their life via taking lots of medication. This "disorder" is of course a good sign or stage relative to no sense of time perception dimension, any human being that got the written education and has not applied the remedy and shows no symptoms of depression outwardly tends to be fatalities to the education. Another way to look at it is their mind is bending so far to the left they will go through their whole life and never show any signs of right brain unveiling. They tend to be people who were brought up very strictly and they are very afraid and very careful to never take any chances so their mind has been permanently frozen by the education. This is all relative to the reverse thing. Depression and suicidal thoughts are a good sign and no depression or suicidal thoughts are a bad sign relative to right brain traits unveiling after all the left brain favoring education. Blessed are the poor in spirit which means the depressed and suicidal because they have a chance to unveil right brain aspects after education veils them.

1:35:24 PM – Failure seldom disappoints like victory does.

"What it comes down to is that modern society discriminates against the right hemisphere."
- Roger Sperry (1973) Neurobiologist and Nobel Lauriat

[modern society(left brain influenced adults that got the education and have not applied the remedy) discriminates against the right hemisphere(children that have yet to get the education so they still have right brain traits active in the conscious state)]

What is, is what a person understands and what will be is what a person wills.

This is a comment on a web site and it is relative to a misspelling where the user actually has an aversion to a misspelling or a compulsion.

"Aye, sometimes I have pet peeves and this site is the cause of one. The pet peeve I'm referring to is the spelling of encyclopedia on the home page (it is currently spelled as encyclopaedia). If a mod could please fix this that would be greatly appreciated. Lately it's been keeping me up at night thinking how this misspelling could go unnoticed for so long."

This is a symptom of being in the extreme left brain state where a person notices parts and when they perceive the parts are improper it bothers them mentally. They have a very strong compulsion relative to "good and evil". The person perceives this [encyclopaedia] is improper, evil, bad and some symptoms of that are [Lately it's been keeping me up at night thinking how this misspelling could go unnoticed for so long.] The person may not actually be losing sleep but the simple fact they made a post to get the "evil" corrected shows it was bothering them. Perhaps every time this person logged into the web site they checked to see if the word was still misspelled and that may very well be because they see "good and evil" and that is a compulsion and a control aspect. So this aversion built up in their mind until they had to make a post about it. They could no longer stand that "evil" misspelled word on the front page of the web site. This suggests stress is being caused because this person see's "good and evil".

[Genesis 2:17 But of the tree of the knowledge of good and evil, thou shalt not eat of it: for in the day that thou eatest thereof thou shalt surely die.]

Once a person gets that education their mind favors left hemisphere so much they see "good and evil" or many parts and this causes stress among other things. Now an English teacher may see this word [encyclopaedia] and think "That is a bad spelling and it shows a person is not wise and shows a person is not well educated." When in reality is does not mean that at all. This [encyclopaedia] does not mean anything at all relative to good or evil, wise or stupid, intelligence or retardation; it is factually marks arranged in an order that suggests an idea or ideal. Some will suggest it is not professional to have misspelled words but they do not even know what professional is.

Professional: conforming to the standards of skill, competence, or character normally expected of a properly qualified and experienced person in a work environment.

Professional is in fact conformity and conformity is what a person seeks if they never wish to be labeled this [Conduct Disorder] or this [criminal] or this [outcast] or this [revolutionary]. So professional is relative to conformity so it is a nice way to say follow the herd and above all do not think for yourself. There is a comment that suggests too many chiefs and not enough Indians. That is saying "herd mentality is best" and that is saying "let others think for you" and that is totally contrary to how a being with right brain traits unveiled thinks because they have massive intuition and pattern detection relative to a person with right brain traits veiled. That's a nice way of saying I don't need a herd because I can think for myself now and although that herd may have an aversion to that concept it is only because they cannot think for their self. This is the reverse thing.

Vigilante: somebody who punishes lawbreakers personally rather than relying on the legal authorities.

This person is a vigilante.

[The pet peeve I'm referring to is the spelling of encyclopedia on the home page (it is currently spelled as encyclopaedia). If a mod could please fix this that would be greatly appreciated.]

He is saying "you have broken a rule and I am punishing you by posting on your forum so everyone can see you broke a rule and that should "scare" you enough to conform to my desire to amend for breaking the rule." There are very subtle suggestions of fear tactics in his comments.

[If a mod could please fix this that would be greatly appreciated.] This is saying "Do what I say and it will please me." This vigilante has the might of the scribes on his side. No scribe on this planet would suggest this is the proper spelling for the word in question: [encyclopaedia]. An English teacher is a vigilante as well as a math teacher because all they do all day long is [punishes lawbreakers] which are the children. When a child gets a math problem wrong they are punished by the vigilante with bad grades and if they are punished enough with bad grades it will influence their entire life and eventually the child will get the impression they have bad genes or a bad mind and they start to settle for slave crap jobs because they listened to a neurotic fool that assumed they understood what intelligence is. Some of the more intelligent children detect hell when they see it and determine it is best to leave swiftly.

[S. H. (16) brought a gun to school and shot himself because of bad grades.]

So who are the [legal authorities] relative to spelling and grammar and math? No one is and at the exact same time everyone is. Some beings that are mentally unsound and only see good and evil will tell a child they are evil or bad or stupid because they cannot spell this word [encyclopaedia] properly and some beings that are mentally sound would never tell a child the inability to spell said word properly is an indication of intelligence or lack of intelligence or reflects upon the child's genes. That's a nice way of saying I can use the language properly but I know it may drive certain scribes mad when they see all the "evil" broken laws in my books relative to grammar so I attempt to edit the books as little as possible to inflict maximum mental harm on them. On the other hand I am also conditioning them to be less compulsive about details and thus they favor right brain because they are forced to overlook all the details and focus on the concepts or the spirit of what is suggested. It is not logical a sound minded human being would be mentally harmed by characters or marks that are perceived to be out of sequence but it is logical a being that see's way too many parts would have a great aversion to anything they perceive it out of what they assume is order. Right brain deals with random access left brain deals with linear aspects or sequential aspects. Sequence suggests order and random access suggests chaos. It is logical a person in extreme left brain state would be displeased with chaos and so it is logical they would seek to control or manipulate situations to restore a sort of perceived linear or an orderly environment. For example:

"Clean up your room it is a mess."

Mess: a chaotic, confused, or troublesome state or situation.

A mess is a confused state or situation so it is logical a person with right brain random access traits veiled would have trouble with those situations. The scribes have trouble with the unknown because the unknown is chaotic and confused relative to their perception. What that means is the scribes need as much order or linear aspects as possible and that means they need as many rules and laws as possible so they can avoid the unknown or chaotic situations. This leads to a situation where a person has their entire life based on rules and laws and they perceive as long as they follow those rules and laws they will perhaps avoid the unknown or the chaotic completely. That is a nice way of saying the scribes become confused in chaos and so the more rules and laws they have the less chaos they have to deal with and thus the less confused they become. It is elementary logic that a person with right brain traits veiled would not be able to tolerate chaos, confusion, the unknown or messes. As rules and laws increase in number chaos and disorder decreases but so does freedom.

Freedom : a state in which somebody is able to act and live as he or she chooses, without being subject to any undue restraints or restrictions.

Horace Mann. Mann was a brother-in-law to author Nathaniel Hawthorne. In 1852, Massachusetts passed the first compulsory education laws and by about 1920 all states had compulsory education laws and this is when this stopped happening [a state in which somebody is able to act and live as he or she chooses, without being subject to any undue restraints or restrictions.]

If one applies the reverse thing in this situation, Horace Mann is a great man relative to everyone getting written education and if one reverses that he is perhaps the worst man in the history of America because he started a movement that robbed everyone of their [ability to act and live as he or she chooses, without being subject to any undue restraints or restrictions.] Written education factually hinders the mind of a child and this man passed a law in his state that soon spread to all states so he ensured all children in America would have their mind hindered by law knowingly or unknowingly. It of course is not so much about the education as it is about not telling anyone is has potentially bad mental side effects when taught to children whose minds do not develop until they are perhaps twenty five and then that compounded with the fact the remedy to the bad mental side effects is never mentioned and that can only be the result of one of two things. Someone is knowingly wanting everyone to be mentally hindered or someone is unaware they are mentally hindering any human being that gets this education starting nearly twenty years before their mind even develops. So this Horace Mann perhaps had good intentions and perhaps the first human being that invented written language and math had good intentions as well but that means less than nothing. So America was founded in 1776 and it went on for nearly one hundred years until written education became law or compulsory. The scribes have this concept that if one gets education they are better or wiser and they get better jobs but the reality is the vast majority of children that get this education end up with jobs they hate. What this suggests is education itself means very little because there are never enough "good jobs" to begin with. If the good jobs were too plentiful then they would not be good jobs. There has to be crap jobs to give contrast to suggest good jobs. This is the proper definition of a job. [a criminal act, especially a robbery]

A person is born. They are forced by law to get the written education starting at seven. It favors the left hemisphere and one is punished for not doing well at it so they in turn hinder their right brain traits to get rewards. They then graduate and depending on how well they did they get a job that many perhaps do not even like and so they are robbed of their purpose in life because they are stuck with a ten percent mind and also a job that they hate. It is a criminal act to harm a child and the written education certainly mentally devastates a child and I know that is a fact because I was one of them and it nearly killed me and then it is a crime to put a human being in a situation they have to slave at a job they hate just so they can get food and water because the control structure has a monopoly on the food and water supplies. So a child goes to school and gets a job [a criminal act, especially a robbery] done to their mind and then they get a job [[a criminal act, especially a robbery] they are not pleased with and pretty much their entire life is a waste and their genius mind is destroyed and they are stuck in the place of sorrow, hell and their chance of even applying the remedy to get their mind back is slim. I apologize I am infinitely beyond your understanding. - 4/21/2010 9:23:00 PM

4/22/2010 9:24:54 AM – Hope is a nice way of saying ignorance; grief is a nice way of saying acceptance. As fear and panic increases mental clarity decreases so fear is a tyrant's best ally. If one explores the reverse concept one may notice the ones that appear least important are most important and things that appear least important are most important and then one may begin to detect many illusions.

[Matthew 26:51 And, behold, one of them which were with Jesus stretched out his hand, and drew his sword, and struck a servant of the high priest's, and smote off his ear.

Matthew 26:52 Then said Jesus unto him, Put up again thy sword into his place: for all they that take the sword shall perish with the sword.]

[Then said Jesus unto him] is out of sequence a sign post that right brain random access was factoring into the writer of this texts it "should" be [Then Jesus said Unto him] The words "Jesus" and "said" are out of sequence. This is what speaking in tongues is, just speaking in random access at times but relative to the persons perception doing the speaking it appears proper but relative to a person that has right brain aspects veiled, a scribe, it appears "odd".

These comments are relative to this loss of ego that occurs after one applies the remedy and is also relative to this concept of protecting the ark of the covenant.

[And, behold, one of them which were with Jesus stretched out his hand, and drew his sword] This is a being that understood Jesus did in fact understood the covenant which is the remedy to the tree of knowledge and understood it well and he was attempting to protect Jesus. The complexity is a being in sound mind has no ego or pride so they are not seeking to defend their pride and that means they are not seeking to defend their life from the scribes.

[for all they that take the sword shall perish with the sword.]

This disciple should have ignored Jesus and protected him because a being with no ego is like a child and does not seek to protect their self. So this disciple was correct in protecting Jesus and Jesus with no ego or pride was in line with not attempting to save himself, an indication he had no ego or sin, pride.

This comment is also saying relative to that time period, "If you apply the remedy and attempt to fight the scribes they will wipe you off the map." The deeper reality is even if you verbally give your testimony they will perhaps still wipe you off the map and that is relative to this comment [Luke 10:3 Go your ways: behold, I send you forth as lambs among wolves.] This comment is saying "Do the best you can to give your testimony after you apply the remedy before the scribes lock you in jail or butcher you." This concept is not even perhaps possible unless a being has no fear, no pride and no ego at all because if they do they will hide or keep their mouth shut or run. These are some patterns relative to this submission to death or harm even though one is just telling the truth.

[Xenophon and Plato agree that Socrates had an opportunity to escape, as his followers were able to bribe the prison guards.] – Wikipedia.com

[Socrates had an opportunity to escape] The reason Socrates did not try to escape was because he had no ego. Another way to look at it is he saw himself as nothing as he suggested.

"As for me, all I know is that I know nothing." - Socrates

Jesus certainly could have run and hid and perhaps could have even said "Protect me from the scribe minions that have come to get me." But instead he said [Put up again thy sword into his place] which is a symptom of humility or lack of ego. One way to look at it is, Socrates was simply suggesting there were problems with the written education relative to it harms the mind and he was killed for that but it is true and so he factually on an absolute scale did nothing wrong , he told the truth and he was killed for it. Jesus also factually did not do anything wrong but tell the truth and he was killed for it.

[Matthew 26:57 And they that had laid hold on Jesus led him away to Caiaphas the high (scribe) priest, where the scribes and the (scribe)elders were assembled.]

It is one thing to come out and say asbestos harms people and that can be understood and corrected and very little adjustment is needed and it may not affect very many people but it is another thing to say "All written education and math taught to young children factually ruins their mind completely and the remedy is very harsh." That is the whole point of all of this, the ones that applied the remedy gave their testimony because they had no ego, they had no fear of death and the proof is, they were fully aware the end result would be death at the hands of the scribes. Everyone has to eventually attempt to be a human being and face the reality of what these written inventions have done to our species. These beings were simply saying "I am aware there are problems with the tree of knowledge, written language and I even have the remedy to its mental damage and so perhaps you should rethink pushing it on the children so carelessly" and the ruler scribes said "Kill that being because if what he is saying is true the common people will have our heads on a stake." I am not saying you have to apply this remedy, in fact many simply cannot because they are mental fatalities or they are their own worst enemies, because it is your business, but I am certain if you do apply this remedy you will come to a new understanding relative to what Goliath and his armies means.

Goliath = [(scribe)elders; control structure]

Goliath Armies = [the scribes; law enforcement; military, judges]

Perhaps I should be depressed but the concept of focus on the log in your eye is one takes anything that is before them and uses it to better their understandings. This means one says what is on their mind to the scribes and then they seek further understandings from the response. It is very risky.

[1 Corinthians 4:10 We are fools for Christ's sake, but ye are wise in Christ; we are weak, but ye are strong; ye are honourable, but we are despised.]

"We" = the ones that applied the remedy and restored right brain aspects.

"are fools" = relative to the reverse thing. It is very foolish to tell scribes their script ruins the mind of the children it is very foolish to tell the truth to the sinister that hates the truth; it is very foolish to show the light to the darkness because the darkness cannot stand the light and must kill it or be consumed by the light.

[for Christ's sake] = Jesus explained his version of the remedy "Deny yourself" and "those who lose their life (mindfully) preserve it." and these (disciples) beings applied it. So this comment is saying "We only woke up from the neurosis because we listened to what Jesus told us to do." relative to drop your nets and apply the remedy.

Drop your nets and follow me is relative to this comment = [Mark 8:34 And when he had called the people unto him with his disciples also, he said unto them, Whosoever will come after me, let him deny himself, and take up his cross, and follow me.]

Let him deny himself the full measure is the remedy so in order to follow Jesus you had to deny yourself. = [let him deny himself, and take up his cross, and follow me.]

[Genesis 1:10 And God called the dry land Earth; and the gathering together of the waters called he Seas: and God saw that it was good.]

Earth and Sea = good = no prejudice.

Perhaps this is suggesting God has no prejudice so we are left to our own devices. If we want to mentally hinder everyone and destroy the whole planet and kill each other and harm each other and ruin everything God perhaps sees that as "is". Perhaps you want to pray to God to cure you of cancer but perhaps God see's your death by cancer as "is"? Perhaps you want God to kill your enemy but what if God see's your enemy as "is"? Perhaps you want to pray to God to give you money but perhaps God see's your lack of money as "is". Perhaps this existence is just an experiment and God does not alter his experiment once it is started because God does not see his experiment needs altering so therefore we are left to our own devices. Perhaps the amount of control you have been given scares you. Perhaps the amount of control you have been given has started to control you. A being that has no prejudice see's everything as one thing, as is. If you want to talk supernatural you remember you ate off the tree of knowledge and you have not applied the remedy so it is infinitely probable the only thing you pray to is the four headed ram.

[Genesis 3:14 And the LORD God said unto the serpent(the four headed ram god, the scribe), Because thou hast done this(got the written education and did not apply the remedy), thou art cursed(has right brain aspect veiled; separated from the God image in man and thus God) above all cattle(dumber than a rock), and above every beast of the field; upon thy belly shalt thou go, and dust shalt thou eat all the days of thy life:]

I have lots of prejudice. I don't like human beings that mentally rape children into hell and then suggest they do not. I do not like human beings that mentally rape children into hell and then suggest there is going to be peace. I live in a country where one has the absolute freedom of speech and no matter what if anyone attempts to stand in the way of freedom of speech it is my right to alter or abolish them and I am infinitely pleased with that understanding.

[that whenever any Form of Government(control structure or person) becomes destructive(abridges freedom of speech) of these ends, it is the Right of the People(Me) to alter or to abolish it,] - Constitution

Abolish: to put an end to something.

I am pleased I have the right to put an end to something. I want you to judge me so I can sit here and laugh at how delusional your attempts to label me are. Relative to my perception I get you for infinity and you get me for the rest of the time. They found a new kind of slug today that shoots love darts and I have to write a book to clarify that one. I am approachable from a distance, an infinite distance.

4/22/2010 4:38:14 PM – I quit.

4/23/2010 4:45:02 AM – Fear not denotes avoiding emotions and the strongest emotion is fear. Fear is relative to the hypothalamus. A fight or flight response is relative to fear and that is what the hypothalamus gives, fight or flight responses. You go on a job interview and you may say certain things certain ways because you fear you may not get the job. You may be in sales and most jobs are relative to sales directly or indirectly and so you may say certain things certain ways because you fear losing a customer. Imagine if a leader told you exactly what was on their mind without any reservations relative to fear. Most leaders tell you what is on the paper not what is on their mind and the reason for that is fear. Fear of misspeaking. The world of the scribes is based on giving off the impression one never makes a mistake. Relative to the sense of time perception dimension a mistake is looked at like a weakness. Contrary in the no sense of time perception dimension everything is looked at like an opportunity to come to a further understanding. This attempt to never make a "mistake" creates lots of stress and anxiety. "I don't want to say anything I will regret." In order for a person to be in that state of mind they have to have a great deal of ego or pride. If one flips the comment it comes out as "I want to say things I won't regret." So there is some sort or perceived value to saying something one won't regret and so there is disvalue relative to regret. This suggests regret or shame is relative to fear or danger. A person can regret what they said and also regret what they avoided saying. This does not apply to the machine state because one simply looks at comments as "things" and no so much as "good or bad" and this is relative to the right brain holistic outlook but even deeper one does not recall details as well as they recall concepts. In the machine state one day is perceived to be a very long time and not long at the same time so one may have a conversation in the morning and by the evening that conversation is perceived to have happened a long time ago and so only concepts of that conversation are remembered. Contrary, the sense of time perception dimension means things are happening very fast so a conversation in the morning is recalled very well in the evening. What this creates is a perception that the conversation is continuing. For example a person with a sense time of time speaks to someone in the morning and then in the evening and it does not seem like much time has passed so it seems like it is on ongoing conversation and contrary in the machine state every conversation is a completely new conversation because one can only operate in real time. It is difficult perhaps to speak with fear when one is in the machine state because fear denotes future expectations. "If you say that, something bad will happen." Bad is relative. "will happen" suggests future tense.

Fear: an unpleasant feeling of anxiety or apprehension caused by the presence or anticipation of danger.

Anxiety: nervousness or agitation, often about something that is going to happen.

Danger: exposure or vulnerability to harm, injury, or loss.

Anxiety creates stress and stress creates fatigue so as anxiety decreases mental clarity increases. Agitation is another way of saying aversion.

Aversion: a strong feeling of dislike of somebody or something. The more aversions you have to things the more anxiety you have and the more agitation you have and the more stress you have and the less mental clarity you have. Danger is relative to perceived loss so the less one has an aversion to loss the better. The more a person perceives potential loss prospects the more they fear and the more anxiety they have. A person may not say what is on their mind because they fear they may lose their friends and so attachment or desire to have friends may lead one to keeping their thoughts to their self so one is accepting censorship for friendship. This suggests the less friends one has the less they censor their thoughts or comments. The more friends a person has the more they have to "watch" what they say. They may say one thing around all their friends and then they fear they may lose friends and that danger is perhaps too scary for some to deal with. "If you say that to that person they will not like you anymore." That is censorship based on fear. This perhaps suggests what a person says or thinks is not as important as keeping friends. That suggests a person is not as important as the friends they keep. That is relative to ego and pride. The only beings in the sense of time perception dimension that do not care about friends are the depressed and suicidal because they are isolating their self and in fact in a state of mental "mediation" and detachment. Depressed people tend to mediate on loss. Depressed people tend to weight their own worth and weigh how much they have to lose. Suicidal people are mindful of death and death is loss. Everything must be detached from or let go of mindfully in order for a suicidal person to "pull the trigger" so to speak. The moment a suicidal person determines there is nothing worth holding on to they tend to commit suicide and so depression is the attempt to confront loss and suicide is the achievement or the realization one is able to let go or deal with loss, absolute detachment. The deeper reality is, this detachment aspect is nothing but a symptom right brain is attempting to come back to the middle or to the conscious state. Another way to look at it is once one applies the remedy the full measure they are never able to become depressed again because they have made their peace with absolute loss, death, in applying the remedy. With right brain random access in the conscious state, a mindful state of depression or any prolonged emotional aspect is factually impossible because the thoughts are coming and going at swift speeds and are random. So depression itself is simply a symptom of the absence of the right brain random thoughts from the conscious state. One might look at it like a person in the sense of time perception dimension has a very prolonged emotional capacity in contrast to one that is in the no sense of time perception dimension. Antidepressants do not make ones thoughts random access so in fact they are not going to ever cure the depression they are just going to alter the persons mental state and then when they wear off the person is depressed again because depression is a symptom the right brain random access thoughts are no longer active in the conscious state so one has a very pronounced emotional capacity. Not suggesting a conspiracy but it certainly is a large money making opportunity for the makers of antidepressants. Applying the remedy is an intangible mental exercise and then one can never be depressed so there is no money to make at it and that is perhaps very bad news for some. This concept of random access shifting thoughts applies to any kind of "compulsion" or "addiction" or "prolonged mental state". If one cannot maintain a mental state of addiction or compulsion then it is not possible for them to have one and that is why right brain random access is so powerful relative to mental well being.

Random: done, chosen, or occurring without an identifiable pattern, plan, system, or connection.

No identifiable pattern in the thoughts. This certainly is perceived to be dangerous to ones that are use to linear left brain thoughts because it makes it very hard for one in the sense of time perception dimension to label a person with no identifiable patterns in their thoughts. A person may say "you are happy." Then say "you are sad" then say "you are angry" then say "You are depressed " then say "You are funny" in the span of about twenty minutes relative to the clock and be completely confused about all these traits and come to the conclusion "That person is mentally ill." This is relative to the concept unnamable or without labels. A person in the sense of time perception dimension tends to seek absolutes and a person in the no sense of time perception dimension tends to seek probabilities. How would one describe how they feel when their thoughts are occurring without an identifiable pattern swiftly? A person in the sense of time perception dimension will suggest absolutes "I am good." 'I am bad." 'I am happy." I am depressed." Those labels cannot happen when ones thoughts are occurring without an identifiable pattern and the random thoughts are happening lightning fast relative to a clock. Perhaps up to four or five pattern changes within just a couple of minutes relative to a clock. Perhaps many psychologists in the sense of time perception dimension would say "That is a mental illness." And that is why this being said this : "What it comes down to is that modern society discriminates against the right hemisphere." - Roger Sperry (1973) Neurobiologist and Nobel Lauriat

4/23/2010 4:18:31 PM – Enuresis – This is a behavior disorder commonly known as bed wetting. Some patterns associated with this and this includes children between the age of six and sixteen and is not associated with an actual medical condition:

Limited Social Interaction.
Lower Self-Esteem.
Rejection by Peers.
Anger/Punishment by Parents.
Behavior Problems/Conduct Problems.
Underachievement in School.

All of these aspects are related to the underachievement in school. Underachievement in school causes low self esteem and low self esteem causes limited social interaction and limited social interaction is relative to rejection by peers and underachievement in school causes punishment by parents and that is associated with behavior problems. Another way to look at it is once the left brain favoring education starts around the age of six and perhaps before the anxiety and emotions start to get turned up and this bed wetting is relative to anxiety and emotions. Essentially the child cannot handle the emotions being turned up or the emotional capacity being turned up so swiftly. Think about a situation that may cause stress or nervousness for example like a big meeting or a situation where one has to speak in front of people or any number of situations where one becomes anxious and nervous and then has to go to the bathroom. That is abnormal and related to this condition and is a symptom of the neurosis caused by the written education. One way to look at it is the remedy is to get the hypothalamus to give the strongest signal it can the death signal and then ignore it and if one can achieved that they no longer have self esteem issues and they also are unable to become stressed over social interaction. It seems that society has issues with people with low self esteem but they prefer that to a person with an infinite self esteem because they call that person egotistical and stuck up so perhaps society is confused about what is the natural or normal mental state one should be in. Rejection by peers has a lot to do with not following the crowd. I am the master of rejection by peers all the sudden but that does not give me self esteem issues because I am mindful the beings in the sense of time perception dimension have their intuition as well as many right brain traits veiled so they have trouble thinking for their self. This conduct problem keeps coming up in many of these "disorders" and it shows a control aspect. Sometimes a parent will say "If you did as I told you this would not have happened." or "If you would have done better in school you would not be in this situation." And this is the peer pressure put on a being to get the left brain conditioning and also the willingness to be controlled aspect that comes along with it. A person is bad or has a mental disorder if they prefer to think for their self is along the lines of societies premise. "Get in line like everyone else or you are mentally ill." A depressed person is actually thinking for their self and that is why they isolate their self, essentially they are attempting to separate from the herd mentality and of course they are labeled [Limited Social Interaction]. Many of the great minds in history had limited social interaction and were what one might consider hermits and it has a lot to do with contact. Another way to look at it is once one applies the remedy their intuition and awareness returns to normal and that is very powerful relative to a person in the sense of time perception dimension and this neurosis is apparent and it is draining on them. It is really the disconnect in the two perception dimensions so the two dimensions do not mix well but also in the sense of time perception dimension one tends to seek peer acceptance and will do many things to get that and contrary in the no sense of time perception dimension one is not looking for peer acceptance or is not affected by lack of peer acceptance because one is in the machine state and acceptance denotes future expectations. That's a nice way of saying the scribes dislike of me breaks my heart. One seeks acceptance but that is not realistic in the machine state. One way to look at this Enuresis condition is one does not piss their pants after they apply the remedy because their hypothalamus is not wacked out any longer so this condition in children is a symptom the hypothalamus is starting to become wacked out as a result of being around people in the sense of time perception dimension, ones that got the education and did not apply the remedy, and also from getting the education itself. On another level in the machine state one cannot maintain a mental state of anxiety or stress for any period of time in contrast to a being in the sense of time perception dimension. If one cannot maintain a mental state of stress one cannot maintain a mental state of anxiety, thus one cannot maintain a mental state of nervousness, one cannot maintain a mental state of low self esteem but this is all achieved because right brain random access thoughts are not veiled and they are thus constantly occurring without an identifiable pattern.

Expressive Language Disorder: The scores obtained from standardized individually administered measures of expressive language development are substantially below those obtained from standardized measures of both nonverbal intellectual capacity and receptive language development. The disturbance may be manifest clinically by symptoms that include having a markedly limited vocabulary, making errors in tense, or having difficulty recalling words or producing sentences with developmentally appropriate length or complexity.

This disorder is so discriminatory against right brain it actually is the left brain influenced beings hate anyone that has right brain aspects unveiled and they do that because they have their right brain aspects silenced so right brain aspects look alien to them. Deeper reality is misery loves company.

[making errors in tense] This is relative to sense of time. If a person has no sense of time then obviously errors in tense of words is going to happen and tense requires judgment. This is relative to the holistic aspect of right brain and that means one is not a good judge or one has no prejudice. This all comes back to this fact: [modern society discriminates against the right hemisphere.] Modern society are human beings that got all the left brain favoring education and now they are extreme left brain influenced and they have not applied the remedy and they discriminate against any being that does apply the remedy or any group of beings that never got the education such as tribes or natives. Black tends to see white as black. The darkness tends to see the light as darkness. Insanity tends to see sanity as insanity. This disorder focuses on one's ability to use the language properly and that premise is built on the assumption written language or language in general has no flaws. One can say about me you cannot use commas properly, tense properly, paragraphs properly and that proves you are mentally ill and I can turn around and say the fact you can use all those prejudice and judgmental aspects properly proves beyond a shadow of a doubt your right brain holistic aspects are everything in the universe but factoring into your perception. It all comes down to a contest and if the contest is about who can think for their self I win and if the contest is about who can assume pack mentality better the scribes win. One might suggest the first forty years of my life I came to understand the scribes are clueless and for the rest of infinity I attempt to explain why. Simply put this [making errors in tense] is discrimination against the holistic aspect of right brain but society will never admit that because they are the discriminator. The scribes have been knowingly or unknowingly conditioned to hate an entire aspect of their mind and the complex powerful aspect at that. I don't use the word discriminate I use to the word hate. The scribes hate the god image in man. For example a treatment for this [making errors in tense} is:

In addition to special classroom instruction at school, students with learning disorders frequently benefit from individualized tutoring which focuses on their specific learning problem.

[individualized tutoring which focuses on their specific learning problem.] All this is saying is a student will get extra help in assisting them to veil that troubling right holistic aspect that still factors into that child's perception which will cure their inability to use tense properly. [Insert spitting blood comments here.] One cannot be more of a self hater than to actually have institutional structures build around the premise that right brain aspects must be veiled or silenced and what is spooky is the scribes do not even know that is what they are doing. There are some examples in history where a people have been conditioned to hate something so much it slowly becomes proper to hate that thing.

Hate: to dislike somebody or something intensely, often in a way that evokes feelings of anger, hostility, or animosity.

What is comes down to is modern society has anger, hostility, and animosity towards right hemisphere. Most control freaks wield control under the guise of authority because they have no true authority relative to ability to direct others without using fear tactics. There is no worse tragedy than when beings that sense time come to a conclusion. I can't dumb myself down to your level I can only dumb you up to mine.

4/23/2010 11:10:45 PM – [Titus 1:15 Unto the pure all things are pure: but unto them that are defiled and unbelieving is nothing pure; but even their mind and conscience is defiled.]

[Unto the pure all things are pure] = the pure are the ones who apply the remedy and are of sound mind and the characteristic of this is [all things are pure] which is a holistic perspective relative to this comment: [Genesis 1:10 And God called the dry land Earth; and the gathering together of the waters called he Seas: and God saw that it was good.]. God see's everything as one thing or as good and the pure also see everything is pure or good which is a holistic aspect and right brain see's holistically and a being of sound mind which both hemispheres are 50% see's holistically because in a sound mind situation right brain traits are the more powerful.

[but unto them that are defiled and unbelieving is nothing pure;]

[but unto them that are defiled]

Defiled : to corrupt or ruin something.

This is what causes the defilement:

Y = "In humans, the frontal lobe reaches full maturity around only after the 20s, marking the cognitive maturity associated with adulthood" - Giedd, Jay N. (october 1999). "Brain Development during childhood and adolescence: a longitudinal MRI study". Nature neuroscience 2 (10): 861-863.

Z = " If you reflect back upon our own educational training, we have been traditionally taught to master the 3 R's: reading, writing and arithmetic -- the domain and strength of the left brain" -
The Pitek Group, LLC.
Michael P. Pitek, III

(Z) factored in with the reality (Y) = defiled which means the mind is ruined, hindered or corrupted. Corrupted or ruined is not an absolute it is a probability and that means although the remedy is perceived to be harsh to apply from the perception of ones that have the corruption it is in actuality not very difficult to apply because it is a one second mental self control exercise.

[defiled and unbelieving is nothing pure] This perhaps is a question although the question mark is missing.

Unbeliever is simply a person that got the written education yet cannot believe it mentally harmed them and that is a logical response since they have no way to tell it harmed them because their mind did not develop until they are 20 to 25 but they got the education at a very young age. I certainly had no idea the education hindered my mind, relative to my perception I was just very depressed and now I understand I was showing end stage symptoms right brain was attempting to unveil and it was a fluke I survived that stage and applied the remedy. Perhaps the most important aspect of belief is proof , this is proof [reading, writing and arithmetic -- the domain and strength of the left brain] and this is complementary proof [In humans, the frontal lobe reaches full maturity around only after the 20s, marking the cognitive maturity] but the catch is the "corruption" hinders ones cognitive ability and thus one's ability to detect proof when they see it.

[is nothing pure] This is a part of that comment that appears to be a question, "Is nothing pure? A person that has right brain holistic aspects veiled see's many parts so if one has one hundred people that are in this corrupt state and they are asked about say ten colors it is probable they will never agree all those colors are "pure". There will be some people who dislike some of the colors but with the "pure" they see holistically so they would see all the colors are "pure" or "good". Pure is not suggesting morals as much as it is suggesting perception or an uncorrupted perception. I am clearly not moralistically pure because I talk to you, although from an infinite distance. This uncorrupted perception means one has to actually apply self control to see parts and so this means one has to ignore this uncorrupted perception in order to speak out against the written education and speak out against the ones that push it with reckless abandon on the children. The thought chain goes something like, all human beings are good, some human beings get the education and become mentally corrupted, those mentally corrupted in turn mentally corrupt their offspring. One is in a situation where they are fully aware the ones mentally corrupted were mentally corrupted as children by mentally corrupted adults so it is not their fault but they continue to corrupt the offspring using the same methods that corrupted them so it is their fault, but they also know not what they do , so it is not their fault, but the children are still being harmed, but the corrupted adults have no cognitive ability relative to complexity so it is not their fault, but they are factually corrupting the offspring so it is their fault. So eventually one has to just throw morals out the window and determine the offspring are more important than the corrupted. So I write because I have determined the offspring are of more value than the adult corrupted which means I have to see parts or have a prejudice but even after that I am not at a stage I will harm the corrupted adults because I still see them without prejudice or as innocent in this situation and this is exactly why the curse this education has caused our species is unstoppable. That is a nice way of saying the only prayer I say is this one: [Jonah 4:3 Therefore now, O LORD, take, I beseech thee, my life from me; for it is better for me to die than to live.]

This also suggests this supernatural assumption is perhaps not even playing a role in this situation at all because we are not corrupting ourselves less with this education in contrast to 5400 years ago when written education was invented we are corrupting ourselves to the infinite degree more. It is not getting better relative to this curse it is only getting worse. A judge once told me "If you want to kill yourself there is nothing anyone can do about it" and I would suggest to the species if you want to kill yourself with this corrupting education there is nothing anyone can do about it. If you want to mentally ruin all the children there is nothing anyone is going to do to stop you, perhaps. So this whole concept about supernatural controlling everything is certainly not panning out in the one situation that matters the most, the mental corruption of the children on an industrial scale by force of law. But the deeper reality is I have determined to stop the scribes from mentally harming the children and they perhaps can test if their prayers to supernatural will protect them from me this time around. I do not give a rat's ass one way or another if I can do it, I have just determined to attempt to do it just to see how powerful this right brain aspect is when at full power. Perhaps we can both come to an understanding relative to seeing if six billion corrupted minds can withstand the storm of one sound mind.

[but even their mind and conscience is defiled.] This again is a comment relative to the mind. Many "religious" beings cannot grasp the mind is relative to the spirit so when one speaks of neurology they assume that has nothing to do with the spirit when in reality the mind and the sprit are the exact same thing. Corrupt mind means corrupt spirit.

Why is it the scribes [mind and conscience is defiled.]?

Because [..; the pen of the scribes is in vain.]

Why is the pen of scribes in vain?

Because [reading, writing and arithmetic -- the domain and strength of the left brain].

In favoring the left brain so much in learning to scribe the right brain aspects are veiled and one of those right brain aspect is intuition and that is relative to conscience or soul and so the [mind and conscience is defiled.] So then one must apply the remedy to get their conscience back because the written education has corrupted it. That a nice way of saying the scribes have a soul as long as your definition of soul is a corrupted soul to the degree they have no soul. Apparently I have determined it is proper to torment beings that have been robbed of their souls and perhaps the soulless should be upset about that even though there is nothing they can do to stop me, perhaps. I am fair enough to explain how the soulless can get their soul back but if they determine that is unwise then they should prepare for eternal tormenting at my right hand. I am pleased on one hand if you determine not to apply the remedy because I have infinite punishments that I do not wish to go to waste. The scribes suggest freedom of speech and freedom of press and I will teach you why that was the scribes greatest misstep.

4/24/2010 12:56:14 AM – Blasphemy: disrespect for God or sacred things.

Sacred things would be the mind, and the god image in man is right hemisphere and this [3 R's: reading, writing and arithmetic -- the domain and strength of the left brain] sins or disrespects the god image in man and so after one does this they must repent which means they must apply the remedy to restore the god image in man. A human is born with a sound mind and that is sacred because the mind is relative to the spirit and body so if one pushes this [3 R's: reading, writing and arithmetic -- the domain and strength of the left brain] by force of law on a child they corrupt the child's sacred mind so they blasphemy and if they go even further and do not even suggest to the being the remedy to that corruption them they enter the realms of diabolical.

Diabolical: extremely cruel or evil; connected with the devil or devil worship.

It is logical a being that is diabolical would not agree with that because diabolic by its very nature means one see's the truth as lies and see's purity as impurity. The scribes see an innocent child and determine we must make that innocent child wise like we are and educate that child with reckless abandon and that suggests they see a perfectly mentally sound innocent child as impure. The scribes have determined every child is impure and needs fixing and education and that means their brand of right brain veiling education and that is why they love their compulsory education law. The scribe's compulsory education law ensures no child ends up with a pure uncorrupted mind and the scribes are pleased with that prospect. I am no longer at the level of ignorance I will tolerate an extremely cruel and evil beast. The scribes in their state of mind are life like but nothing more. I see some of the strategies of others in this world who are awake to a degree attempting to reach the scribes and I attempt to do everything they do in reverse. They have followings and I avoid followings. They have popularity and I stay put in my isolation chamber. They seek acceptance with the scribes and I seek division with the scribes. I don't pander to what I own.

[The Nobel Prize in Literature (Swedish: Nobelpriset i litteratur) is awarded annually, since 1901, to an author from any country who has, in the words from the will of Alfred Nobel, produced "in the field of literature the most outstanding work in an ideal direction"]

Ideal: an excellent or perfect example of something or somebody, or something that is considered a perfect example.

Perfect: complete and lacking nothing essential.

A being that has a sound mind relative to both hemispheres working in perfect harmony is a being that is complete and lacking nothing essential relative to mental faculties. After one gets all of this [3 R's: reading, writing and arithmetic -- the domain and strength of the left brain] they in fact have veiled right hemisphere aspects so they are no longer perfect or they are lacking something essential and that one essential thing the scribes are lacking is the full power of their right hemisphere the god image in man, and that means they are lacking God until they apply the remedy which the ancient texts refer to a keeping the covenant or repenting. One can only repent once and one can only keep the covenant once, neither is a lifelong profession and neither are aspects to make money off of.

Literature: fiction, poetry, drama, and [criticism], that are recognized as having important or permanent artistic value.

Criticism: a spoken or written opinion or [judgment] of what is wrong or bad about somebody or something.

Judgment : an opinion formed or a [decision] reached in the case of a disputed, controversial, or doubtful matter.

A proper judge is a being of sound mind and sound mind is relative to sound cognitive ability. A being that has a sense of time, a scribe, cannot be a proper judge because their mind is not sound and thus their cognitive ability is not sound.

Decision: something that [somebody chooses or makes up his or her mind] about, after considering it and other possible choices.

Every year relative to a calendar the scribes decide to push the left brain favoring education on six year old children and that is a decision but it is not a proper judgment because it is a decision to mentally hinder the child. I was one of those children and so are you.

Sammasambuddhas attain buddhahood, [then decide] to teach others (scribes) the [truth; the tree of knowledge hinders the mind] they have discovered.

Truth: the thing that corresponds to fact or reality.

Reality: something that has real existence and [must be dealt with in real life.]

[must be dealt with in real life.] = [reading, writing and arithmetic -- the domain and strength of the left brain] and [humans, the frontal lobe reaches full maturity around only after the 20s, marking the cognitive maturity.] have devastating mental implications.

The scribes must deal with the above reality and my purpose is to ensure they do deal with the above reality especially if it mindfully kills them.

[Genesis 1:27 So God created man in his own [image], in the image of God created he him; male and female created he them.]

Image : a person or thing bearing a close likeness to somebody or something else.

X = left hemisphere
Y = right hemisphere
Z = [reading, writing and arithmetic -- the domain and strength of the left brain]
A = a person or thing bearing a close likeness to somebody or something else
B = remedy

As (Z) increases (A) decreases because (Y) influence decreases and (X) influence increases.

$X + Z > Y + A = B$

After (X) and (Z) state of mind has been achieved then in order to restore (Y) and (A) (B) must be applied.

Mankind was created perfect mentally speaking, in perfect mental balance but then mankind in seeking to become perfect ruined perfection and became imperfect mentally speaking. One can never improve perfection mentally they can only corrupt it by attempting to improve it.

Perfection: the quality of something that is as good or suitable as it can possibly be.

One cannot do better than mental harmony but this [reading, writing and arithmetic -- the domain and strength of the left brain] favors left brain far too much and thus ruins perfection. There is the remedy but it is proper to not ruin perfection to begin with because then one ends up in a situation where they are creating problems they could just avoid to begin with. When you mindfully kill yourself you will understand you would not have had to do that if only the adult scribes had an ounce of foresight and taught you oral education until your mind was a bit more developed. In your quest to mindfully kill yourself to restore your perfect mind you will learn a valuable lesson in the importance of foresight.

Foresight: the ability to envision possible future problems or obstacles.

Envision: to form a mental picture of something, typically something that may occur or be possible in the future. Ability to envision is relative to open-mindedness, creativity and intuition; that latter two are right brain traits.

The scribes have foresight relative to simple aspects but have no foresight relative to complexity because complexity is a right brain trait.

It is probable since God is perfect and mankind in a perfect state of mind is the god image then mankind would be a mirror image of God in a perfect state of mind and the two would be indistinguishable. So a perfect state of mind is a sound mind and in that state of mind one is the image of God so one only has to determine what is a sound mind and then seek that state of sound mind.

[2 Timothy 1:7 For God hath not given us the spirit of fear(timidity); but of ... sound mind.]

Sound mind is a mind absent of fear or timidity.

[Genesis 15:1 After these things the word of the LORD came unto Abram in a vision, saying, Fear not, Abram: I am thy shield, and thy exceeding great reward.]

[Fear not, Abram] = absence of fear or a method to eliminate fear.

[and thy exceeding great reward] = sound mind = one returns to being the God image which is perfect mind = [in the image of God] = a child of God = a mirror of God. Not greater than God just a mirror image of God and the image of God is perfection because God is perfection.

Perfection: the quality of something that is as good or suitable as it can possibly be.

One cannot be anything more than in perfect harmony mentally, both hemispheres working in equal power relative to lateralization. Once one applies the remedy the full measure they return to perfect lateralization and one indication of this is one loses their ability to mindfully register time. This means if one can mindfully register time they are not in perfect lateralization mindfully. Sense of time = not suitable. No sense of time = suitable.

Suitable: of the right type or quality for a particular purpose or occasion.

Sense of time = lacking quality for a particular purpose. No sense of time = quality for a particular purpose.

Purpose: the reason for which something exists or for which it has been done or made = sound mind relative to lateralization.

Lateralization: the localization of the control center for a specific function, e.g. speech, on the right or left side of the brain.

Perfect lateralization = [No spirit of fear or timidity] = [sound mind.]

The only way to achieve this since fear itself is relative to the hypothalamus is to get the hypothalamus to give its strongest fight or flight signal possible, the death signal, and then one ignores it or is indifferent to it and then the amygdala remembers that and the spirit of fear leaves one and one returns to the perfect lateralization, the written education has thrown them out of, shortly as in days relative to a calendar.

This is a comment speaking about a lawsuit.

[The lawsuit seeks more than $75,000 (£49,000) in compensation for (person's name), who was "humiliated, embarrassed, frightened, intimidated, subject to undeserved shame and suffered severe emotional distress".]

This spirit of this comment is saying [A being was so emotionally unstable because someone said a word to them it will take me infinite books to explain it properly]. This lawsuit was filed because someone said something to this being. No person hit this being they simply said something to this being. So this beings response to a sound was [humiliated, embarrassed, frightened, intimidated, subject to undeserved shame and suffered severe emotional distress"] It is obvious this being got the education and it is obvious this being is perhaps slightly on the dramatic side in their explanation of their emotional distress and I would be in emotional distress if they were not being slightly dramatic. Why would a being admit they became [humiliated, embarrassed, frightened, intimidated] because of spoken words which is a sound? Because of this: $75,000. All paying jobs corrupt the mind. This being would not suggest words caused them to be like this [humiliated, embarrassed, frightened, intimidated] on a world stage for no reason at all, but for this [$75,000], no problem at all. If this being had unlimited food, water and shelter they perhaps would not be attempting to make money by suggesting a word someone said to them caused them to be like this [humiliated, embarrassed, frightened, intimidated]. This being is not suffering [severe emotional distress] because someone said a word to them but because they got this [reading, writing and arithmetic -- the domain and strength of the left brain] and their right brain random access thought patterns are gone so they can achieve a mental state of this [severe emotional distress]. There are all these symptoms that are created by all that left brain favoring education and they are not the problem they are just fruits of the core problem.

[reading, writing and arithmetic -- the domain and strength of the left brain] causes [severe emotional distress] which is suffering relative to [Genesis 3:16 ..., I will greatly multiply thy sorrow...;.. sorrow ...shall rule over thee.] = [who was "humiliated, embarrassed, frightened, intimidated, subject to undeserved shame and suffered severe emotional distress".] over words which are sounds someone said to them. This being heard sounds and emotionally collapsed similar to these beings:

[P. P. (15) hanged herself in a closet after she became a victim of cyber-bullying]

[M. M. (13) hung herself in her closet after becoming the victim of cyber-bullying]

Perhaps that latter being's decided to skip the court proceedings and move right on to the final conclusion: escape the narrow altogether. The former being may get 75,000$ but he is still trapped here and the latter beings escaped. I ponder who you will determine is the wiser of the beings. Do you think sound minded human beings that are 13 kill their self over words or do you think 13 year old human beings that have had their emotional capacity greatly increased because the random access aspects of their thoughts have been reduced to a subconscious level kill their self over words and thus sounds? Words are very powerful to the weak minded. For example if I say "You are a loser", you will read that and that and a sound will be created in your mind and it is the same thing as if I was standing next to you and said that to you. The words are not the problem it is the mental state of the observer of the words.

You perhaps get no emotional response from these letters: aprtsi But you may get an emotional response from these letters: rapist. In factual reality the only difference is the sequential arrangement of the letters has changed. You have not been conditioned to have an emotional response to this letter arrangement: aprtsi, but you have been conditioned to have an emotional response to this letter arrangement: rapist. You have not been conditioned to have an emotional response to this letter arrangement: taedh, but you have been conditioned to have an emotional response to this letter arrangement: death. That is a nice way of saying you perhaps have [severe emotional distress] if someone says the word "death" too much and that is an indication of what all that written education has done to your mind. You perhaps would harm people physically or attempt to take money from them or attempt to lock them in jail if they say certain words simply because you perceive you experience [severe emotional distress] because of sounds. Perhaps you would write me a letter and explain to me what it is like to live in massive hallucination world where you have fallen. Perhaps I stay in my isolation chamber to avoid dealing with the [severe emotional distress] ones. Perhaps that is what you should tattoo on your forehead: [severe emotional distress]. Perhaps if you tattoo [severe emotional distress] on your forehead that action will at least give me an indication you have slightly realistic perceptions.

Distress: hardship or problems caused by a lack of basic necessities.

A basic necessity in life is the full power of right hemisphere aspects in the conscious state and if that is not happening one is in distress and a symptom of that distress is [severe emotional distress].

What it comes down to is that modern society discriminates against right hemisphere and thus modern society is in distress. What it comes down to is that modern society discriminates against right hemisphere and thus modern society is in severe emotional distress. What it comes down to is that modern society is in severe emotional distress and thus discriminates against right hemisphere because of that distress and thus modern society is in very severe emotional distress. What it comes down to is modern society discriminates against right hemisphere, the god image in man, and thus modern society is in severe emotional distress because they are separated from God. You can pick out whichever comment you want because the spirit of each comment is identical.

What it comes down to is modern society discriminates against the God image in man, right hemisphere, and thus modern society, the scribes are the anti-christ. Perhaps now you are experiencing severe emotional distress.

Christ: a savior who will come to deliver God's chosen people.

Chosen: picked out from or preferred to the rest; relative to the wheat being separated from the chaff.

Who are the preferred relative to the no sense of time perception dimension? The answer is the down trodden in the sense of time perception dimension; the least among the sense of time perception dimension beings.

Least: a smaller amount than anything or anyone else; relative to lots of chaff and not much wheat; relative to the only beings on the planet in the sense of time perception dimension that assume they are of lesser value than anything or anyone else are the depressed and suicidal scribes and they are the meek.

[Numbers 12:3 (Now the man Moses was very meek, above all the men(scribes) which were upon the face of the earth.)]

Moses was the least among the scribes so he was most valuable in the no sense of time perception dimension. Moses was the least valuable relative to the sense of time perception world so he was the most valuable relative to the no sense of time perception dimension. Everything is reverse because there are two totally separate perception dimensions happening in one physical dimension.

Dimension: a level of consciousness, existence, or reality.

So physics beings attempt to figure out how to travel to other dimensions and how to do that is right in front of their noses and is in these ancient texts they certainly have read at one time or another in their life and the way one travels to the no sense of time dimension is right here: [Psalms 23:4 ... walk through the valley of the shadow of death (mindfully),(and) ... fear not...] What I find interesting is they perhaps doubt that because it is so simple.

Perhaps the proof is in the pudding. If any being on this planet perceives they cannot travel to another level of consciousness and thus another level of reality permanently by applying this remedy perhaps they should attempt to disprove it.

Theory: abstract thought or contemplation.

Fact: something that can be shown to be true, to exist, or to have happened.

I am not suggesting I have traveled to another level of consciousness by accidentally applying this fear not remedy in theory. I am actually showing you by explanation that the fear not remedy is true, the alternate level of consciousness no sense of time perception reality does exist, and I have arrived here. I am attempting to convince you human beings can in fact travel to alternate levels of consciousness which is what a dimension is and this alternate level of consciousness is real. The complexity is alternate suggests abnormal but in reality the written education transports one to an alternate level of consciousness dimension and this remedy transports one back to the normal level of consciousness dimension which is where all human beings start off at birth.

Opinion: the view somebody takes about an issue, especially when it is based solely on personal judgment.

I am not suggesting this no sense of time dimension travel is based on my personal judgment alone in fact I am suggesting I accidentally traveled here to the place many beings for thousands of years relative to a calendar have traveled. I am not unique, I am one of many. The question is how many beings personal judgments are required to make a fact? The answer is two.

[Matthew 18:20 For where two or three are gathered together in my name, there am I in the midst of them.]

[For where two or three are gathered together] = when two beings apply the remedy they will both go to the no sense of time perception dimension and then it will no longer be an opinion of personal judgment but it will be a fact. Two dimension travel observers are required to verify dimension travel relative to level of consciousness or level of reality travel. If I am the only one that can travel to this dimension then I am an exception but if two can travel here then the fear not remedy is a gateway to normal dimension.

Normal: maintained or occurring in a natural state.

Natural: in accordance with the usual course of nature.

When a human being is born they are in the normal no sense of time perception dimension and then they have contact with beings in the sense of time perception dimension and get the written education and leave the normal perception dimension over a period of time relative to a calendar then they apply the fear not "ritual" and they return to the normal perception dimension. I detect one is unable to return to the abnormal sense of time perception dimension and so this is perhaps why the fear not remedy is relative to detachment. That is actually good news not bad news. What that means is once a being leaves that place of suffering one can never go back there again and so one leaves the infinite cycle of suffering forever simply by applying a one second mental self control exercise known as "fear not" among other names. I detect I am being complacent so I digress.

Complacent: self-satisfied and unaware of possible dangers.

[Pacbox: "Still at it Rohrer? It's nonsense. Give it up. You're argument holds no water and never will. It's made up out of thin air."]
[Your account has been locked for the following reason:
[Agenda of contempt for Christianity & Catholiciasm. This change will be lifted: Never]

Because it is not possible to travel in groups it is important to focus on one's self relative to applying the remedy. The word "travel" suggests a duration of travel relative to time but that word does not quite explain it properly. One way to look at it is after one applies the remedy they have this peace that overcomes them and even the next day they feel this certain peace so that is an indication the travel has begun to the normal no sense of time perception dimension but the actual arrival is when one gets an extreme cerebral "ah ha" sensation and then they lose their sense of time and when that happens one has to start to learn everything over again because they are then in a reverse or opposite dimension. Things that applied in the sense of time dimension no longer apply in the no sense of time dimension.

In the SOTD (sense of time perception dimension) emotional capacity is very prolonged. In the NSOTD(no sense of time perception dimension) emotional capacity is very short in contrast. Keep in mind a dimension is a level of consciousness, existence, or reality. Time is a dimension so No Time is also a dimension.

Time: a dimension that enables two identical events occurring at the same point in space to be distinguished, measured by the interval between the events.

In SOTD hunger is very strong and in contrast hunger is nearly absent in the NSOTD. In SOTD recreational drugs have a very pronounced cerebral effect and in the NSOTD recreational drugs have nearly no cerebral effect. For example a person in NSOTD may get very drunk and then they start to "come down" and they notice this profoundly but in the NSOTD this "come down" is hardly noticed if at all because the "going up" is hardly noticed at all on a cerebral level. One has no hang over because they have no hang under, so to speak. Relative to what goes up must come down so the response is what goes sideways is neutral. In the SOTD one see's many parts and thus has many prejudices and in the NSOTD one has no prejudice so everything appears neutral or just is. In the SOTD food has a very distinctive taste and so one has aversion to certain food and in the NSOTD food taste well but there is no great difference between any food. In the SOTD after taste relative to food is prolonged in contrast to the NSOTD where after taste is short. This is a great benefit if ones mate cannot cook well and deeper still everyone will appear to be a great cook in the NSOTD. Everything tastes like chicken even the chicken but one has lots of ambiguity about what chicken tastes like.

4/24/2010 12:53:30 PM –

Doctrine - http://www.youtube.com/watch?v=NgAJ5DjK_nA

Reveal the summer ice
Sending notification is nice
Deadly fungus it could shut down the game
Middle class tighten the rules for shame

Credibility health effects
Censored after the threat inspects
Producers say despite uproar
Find the foreign property, property store

Boot camp death hopes to fly again
In that place where the wise begins
Just don't rest in that place again
You can't live til you rise again
You must take it, break it, forsake it

Boot camp death tries to fly again
In that place where the lights begin
Just don't rest in that place of sin
You can't breathe til you rise again

Get a new old empty episode
Don't drive wearing your kimono
Under house arrest, Under house arrest
Cracking down in this neutral vest
Under house arrest, under house arrest
Post the video under house arrest
Start the study yet with the health effects
Under house arrest foreign property bet, foreign property bet
Middle class holiday, under house arrest, in the neutral vest
Foreign property bet, foreign property bet

Boot camp death hopes to try again
In the place where the sight begins
Just don't rest in that next of kin
You can't breathe til you rise again

4/24/2010 10:39:55 PM –

Drug: an often illegal and sometimes addictive substance that causes changes in behavior and perception and is taken for the effects.

Psychedelic : relating to, caused by, or describing drugs that generate hallucinations, atypical psychic states, or states that resemble psychiatric disorders.

Atypical: not conforming to the usual type or expected pattern.

Brainwashing: to induce somebody to believe or do something.

Y = Psychedelic = reading, writing and arithmetic -- the domain and strength of the left brain

X = [causes changes in behavior and perception and is taken for the effects]= not conforming to the usual type or expected pattern

Z = Compulsory Education Law = to induce somebody to do something

Induce: to persuade or influence somebody to do or think something = get (Y) or you will not have money or have food or have water or have shelter or have luxury = discrimination and/ or fear tactics.

Discrimination: unfair treatment of one person or group, usually because of prejudice.

Anyone that does not get (Y) or does not get enough of (Y) or does not do well enough at (Y) is treated unfairly or discriminated against.

A child that does not do well at (Y) is given poor grades and in turn is looked down upon by their friends and also their parents.

Y + Z = X

This suggests we certainly may be a drug addicted species and anyone that does not do the drug of choice (Y) is discriminated against and one can look at this just like a child at a party and someone passes them a beer and if that child drinks they are accepted and if they do not drink they become a sort of outcast. This drug (Y) perhaps is a sort of hazing ritual.

Hazing: a mental or physical state or condition when feelings and perceptions are vague, disorienting, or obscured.

Our collective species is engaged in (Y). So civilization itself is one group and although there are countries within that set they are not countries but more like factions of the group of civilization. This suggests civilization or society is a huge cult on a planet wide scale and they take the children and put them through this hazing ritual which is (Y) and we do this as a species simply because we are perhaps addicted to drugs and our greatest drug we have ever come up with is (Y). (Y) takes a while to administer but it is a one dose psychedelic and it lasts for the rest of one's life unless one in this [a mental state or condition when feelings and perceptions are vague, disorienting, or obscured] can escape it by applying the (fear not remedy).

A typical hazing ritual is where a person is applying for membership into an elite group and that group makes them do some disorienting things and if that person can "survive" that they become a member of the "elite" group. This means relative to civilization very few have ever passed the hazing ritual and actually applied the remedy to the full measure.

[Luke 20:46 Beware of the scribes]

Why beware of the scribes? They have this very powerful drug (Y) and it perhaps is a bit too demanding relative to a hazing ritual. The remedy to the drugs (Y) is for one to defeat their fear of death or let go of their life mindfully and absolutely and that is along the lines of what hazing rituals are. "Drink this bottle of liquor.", "Go stay in the woods alone by yourself for 3 days.", "Go into that spooky haunted house by yourself.", "Go steal something or embrace a situation with unknown danger involved.". What this indicates is we are perhaps "bored" as a species which means we are so intelligent we create problems because we have no problems. This is not on an individual level but on a collective species level. Because (Y) is a psychedelic we assume this country is different and that country is different but on a collective species level all of the countries are on the psychedelic and thus all the countries are engaged in the same exact hazing ritual. This suggests the ancient texts (religions) perhaps all over the world were a concerted effort by beings that had discovered the remedy or the escape from the hazing ritual attempting to explain to the entire species that is what was happening. It is not logical the ancient texts would speak so much about the "ill effects of the tree of knowledge" and then explain in detail the "remedy" if the beings in the ancient texts were hostile in nature towards the species. It is more along the lines of a being that negates the psychedelic drug(Y) and then they attempt to suggest the remedy to other beings still on the psychedelic drug but it is very difficult because the beings they were speaking to were in a [a mental state or condition when feelings and perceptions are vague, disorienting, or obscured.]. It is difficult to convince a blind man blindness is abnormal. One pattern in this if one thinks about typical hazing rituals is that it is usually the domain of the males and not so much a female type of activity. So this suggests the males are bored and they take this psychedelic (Y) and then they are not so bored anymore and the females are like "Do not mess with that thing." and the males ignore the females and now here we are 5400 years later and the males still ignore the females and everyone is on the psychedelic (Y) and now even the females are on the (Y) psychedelic. No matter what anyone suggests we are four light years away from the nearest star system and it is perhaps understood there is no earth like planet there so we have no known enemies and so we are infinitely bored and so we are a species that has messed around with a very power and essentially permanent mind altering drug and the world is showing symptoms of that. We run around a kill each other over supernatural and we kill each other over money and land and stupidity and those are all symptoms of beings that are hallucinating and not even close to symptoms of a sound minded being. If you would actually harm someone directly or indirectly physically over land or money or resources you are hallucinating because that is total stupidity. Civilization came about as a result of the written language invention and became controlling and coveting and that is a symptom of the hallucinogenic (Y). One group dislikes another group on a world wide scale and that is a symptom of the hallucinogenic. A person dislikes their neighbor and their kids dislike them but they like their city because they dislike the city next to them, they like their state but only because they dislike the state next to them, they like their country only because they dislike the country next to them. People will suggest "I love America" but then they dislike the state next to them and dislike that states football team and dislikes their colleague at work and dislikes the people they elect to lead them and dislike the government but they also dislike people who dislike the government and they dislike their mate and they dislike their self and wish they could lose a few pounds and they dislike many foreign countries and foreign belief systems and when it all comes down to it, it is a symptom they are hallucinating out of their mind and are mentally disorientated from that (Y) psychedelic they had forced on them as a child. Simply put a human beings cannot function on a psychedelic that essentially never wears off but that is what the entire species is not only on, but they continue to push it on the children and they do not even believe they do that at all. So I accidentally applied the remedy to this psychedelic drug (Y) our entire species has been "messing" with for 5000 years and so I certainly should appear very strange in what I suggest because the vast majority of my fellow human beings are factually tripping on a psychedelic that is more powerful than any drugs ever known to mankind because it actually permanently perhaps alters ones perception to the extent every single perception based aspect of a person while on the drug (Y) is reverse of how a person would be if they negated the drug's effects. The drug (Y) is so powerful relative to altering ones perception one has to actually do what are called (short lasting drugs) like alcohol , pot, cocaine and many others just to feel what it is like to not be on the initial psychedelic (Y) but this also magnifies the initial (Y) drug. This is in line with sometime a person takes lots of say crystal meth and then they have to do another drug to come down. One might do a bunch of crack and then have to smoke pot in order to come down. This suggests drug use itself is a symptom people are trying to take the edge off of the "big" drug they are on (Y), the most powerful psychedelic drug. What this means is society is doing well considering they are tripping out of their minds. They are factually in a completely different perception dimension than they would be if they did not get that drug (Y). Society is like a man who drinks a gallon of vodka and then attempts to get his life in order while intoxicated and it will never work and if you look around at society in general and what society is doing to itself and to the environment one can see this very clearly.

"A casual stroll through the lunatic asylum shows that faith does not prove anything."-Friedrich Nietzsche -German philosopher (1844 - 1900)

What is a philosopher? A human being that in one way or another negated the psychedelic drug (Y). What is a prophet? A human being that in one way or another negated the psychedelic drug (Y).

So this means as a species we put people in this hazing test with (Y) and then many do not do so well in that hazing test and they are punished. A person that does drugs is simply attempting to escape the reality caused by the hazing test that was pushed on them as a child using (Y) and so they are called druggies and losers and fools when in reality the hazing test is quite difficult to escape fully. The wise beings in the ancient texts could explain the entire situation flawlessly and even at that, many still in the neurosis, the scribes, caused by the drug (Y) will laugh and mock and make some witty comments suggesting it is not true because they are infinitely disorientated relative to their perception and their cognitive ability because the hazing drug is so powerful. That's a nice way to say it is okay if you mock what I suggest because I am factually explaining why if one has a strong sense of time it is proof they are tripping on a hallucinogenic more powerful than any known hallucinogenic. Society makes billions of dollars off of prescribing drugs to treat an essentially permanent hallucinogenic drug. It is like drinking a gallon of vodka and then attempting to negate that with two aspirin. If society wishes to pass a law that says it is proper to give children a psychedelic drug (Y) administered at the age of seven that takes nearly ten years to fully administer and once that happens that child may not ever be able to undo those mental effects then I will have to stop writing my books because I will abide by that law but until they do I keep writing and exposing the scribes as hallucinating lunatics that are allowed around children and allowed to make determinations about children and I will never show mercy on them. I was one of those children society pushed that drug (Y) on so society has already used up their nine lives in my book and they get no second chances.

One can contrast how women were treated in America by the male scribes before females started getting the drug (Y) to how the Indigenous tribes of America were treated by the male scribes. The correlation is the indigenous tribes and the females did not get the drug (Y) and were thus discriminated against.

X = extreme left brain state of consciousness caused by the (Y) drug
Z = common recreational drugs or any types of drugs from prescription drugs to caffeine
A = effects relative to the beings behavior
B = A being that has applied the remedy to the (Y) drug

$$X + Z = A$$

This equation shows why society assumes the (Z) drugs are so bad for people relative to their mental state because society assumes the people who take (Z) drugs are not on the (Y) drug. Taking the (Z) drugs while on the (Y) drug is the same situation as mixing drugs, it has probable devastating consequences. A person on (Y) drug drinks caffeine and assumes that cerebral sensation is relative to the sensation of a sound minded human being but in fact it is the sensation relative to a being on the psychedelic drug (Y). So this (Y) drug has magnified the effects of all of the cerebral recreational drugs and thus makes one very prone to become addicted to them. Another way to look at it is a person gets the education and years of it and so they are under the influence of (Y) and so they are factually schizophrenic.

Schizophrenia: a severe psychiatric disorder with symptoms of emotional instability (extreme emotional capacity, prolonged emotions that can last relative to envy, greed, lust), detachment from reality (They sense time, have strong hunger, strong fatigue), and withdrawal into the self (Ego & pride).

So like many psychotropic drugs that cause temporary symptoms of schizophrenia this (Y) drug causes permanent schizophrenia and then when that person takes any recreational drug the effects are magnified.

Drug: an often illegal and sometimes addictive substance. Technically the (Y) drug is not a substance it is actually a conditioning aspect.

Conditioning: a method of controlling or influencing the way people or animals behave or think by using a gradual training process.

The complexity is it has all the side effects of a hallucinogenic drug once the conditioning is achieved. For example if you condition a dog to sit and then you give it a treat you have not mentally hindered the dog. The education is conditioning and creates cerebral effects relative to hallucinogenic drugs and probable permanent effects. So society is determining all the recreational drugs are bad because society is not aware they are really observing the symptoms of the drugs on people that are already on a hallucinogenic drug caused by the conditioning called traditional education.

X = extreme left brain state of consciousness caused by the (Y) drug
Z = common recreational drugs or any types of drugs from prescription drugs to caffeine
A = effects relative to the beings behavior
B = A being that has applied the remedy to the (Y) drug

$$B + Z = A$$

This equation is the effects of the drugs on a person that has negated the effects caused by the (Y) drug and so the effect caused by the (Z) drugs are very mild in contrast to the effects of the same drugs to a person in the (X) state of mind caused by the (Y) conditioning drug. For example caffeine does absolutely nothing after one applies the remedy. Perhaps if one drank 10 cups of coffee swiftly they may feel something relative to cerebral aspects but it is not probable. Nicotine does nothing. Alcohol does some things relative to affecting physical motor skills but even in large quantities it does very little cerebrally in contrast to what it does to a being in the (X) state of mind. A (B) being does not go up from drugs cerebrally so one does not come down. Another way to look at it is there is no euphoria and this indicates the beings in (X) state of mind are not feeling euphoria as much as they are feeling right brain unveiled for the duration the drugs lasts and then when the drug wears off they perceive they come down, but in reality they are just experiencing right brain going back to being veiled and they are going back to being in (X) state of mind. The main problem with taking drugs while on the (Y) conditioned drug is one cannot handle feeling right brain unveiled so swiftly. After one applies the remedy and right brain unveils after about 30 days they will assume they went completely mad and they have a brain tumor and something must be wrong because they have never felt what right brain is like at full power in the conscious state of mind and this takes nearly a year just to get use to. It takes nearly a year to get use to being of sound mind and that is an indication of how powerful the (Y) conditioned drug is. So the (Y) drug takes a number of years to administer (school) and after the antidote is applied takes one nearly a year to get use to not being in that (Y) drug level of consciousness, the sense of time perception dimension. Recreational drugs are essentially meaningless once one applies the remedy which means consciousness or being of sound mind is so pleasing in contrast to how one use to be in the (X) state of mind one can take them or leave them and they really have no value at all. One will do a drug after applying the remedy and discover they do not really do anything in contrast to what they use to do in the (X) state of mind so one tends not to do them and it is really that simple. One will find water does just as much to them as the recreational drugs relative to euphoric effects is one way to look at it. I am not making a statement about drugs as much as I am attempting to explain the contrast relative to the drug's effects relative to a person in the (X) state of mind and a person that has applied the remedy to the (X) state of mind. Even drugs like sugar no longer have their cerebral effects or profound taste effects. This is perhaps why the Native Americans did not have sugar perhaps. This is relative to necessity is the mother of invention which means if recreational drugs do not work they probably won't be recreational drugs. This is also suggesting the entire drug problem relative to society is simply human beings attempting to find ways to firstly escape that extreme left brain state of mind the education put them in and also enjoying the effects of drugs on top of the effects of the (Y) conditioned drug effects. Be mindful if you doubt the spirit of what I am suggesting, you have a grasp on how the remedy is applied so go apply it before you speak and attempt to come to conclusions about the remedy. You are causing great harm in your conditioned induced hallucinogenic state and that is no longer going to be tolerated. If you doubt I am inciting resentment towards the scribes you are not thinking clearly.

Resentment: aggrieved feelings caused by a sense of having been badly treated.

You are either for me or against me. - 5:55:00 AM

4/25/2010 6:54:44 AM –

[Psalms 23:4 .. walk through the valley of the shadow of death, (and).. fear no evil:(Then).. thou (will unveil right hemisphere, the god image in man)art with me; thy rod and thy staff they comfort me.]

[Luke 17:33 ..; and whosoever shall lose his life(mindfully) shall (unveil right hemisphere, the god image in man)preserve it.]

[Mark 8:34 ...., he said unto them, Whosoever will come after me, let him deny himself, and take up his cross, and follow me.]

[Whosoever will come after me, let him deny himself] = [whosoever shall lose his life(mindfully) shall (unveil right hemisphere, the god image in man)preserve it.]

[Genesis 15:1 After these things the word of the LORD came unto Abram in a vision, saying,[Fear not], Abram:(then will unveil right hemisphere, the god image in man) = .. exceeding great reward.]

Get into a situation where the hypothalamus gives one the shadow of death signal and then [fear not]
Get into a situation where the hypothalamus gives one the shadow of death signal and then [fear no evil]
Get into a situation where the hypothalamus gives one the shadow of death signal and then [lose your life mindfully]
Get into a situation where the hypothalamus gives one the shadow of death signal and then [let go]
Get into a situation where the hypothalamus gives one the shadow of death signal and then [submit]
Get into a situation where the hypothalamus gives one the shadow of death signal and then [yield]
Get into a situation where the hypothalamus gives one the shadow of death signal and then [bow]
Get into a situation where the hypothalamus gives one the shadow of death signal and then [deny yourself]
All of these methods are methods to negate the mental neurosis caused by the left brain favoring written education and math.

4/25/2010 10:52:13 AM - What you do with information is more important than what you think about it. Not going all the way with the remedy can be as bad as not attempting it.

The way the truth and the life

The way to what?
The way to negate the effects caused by the tree of knowledge relative to:

[
Y = "In humans, the frontal lobe reaches full maturity around only after the 20s, marking the cognitive maturity associated with adulthood" - Giedd, Jay N. (october 1999). "Brain Development during childhood and adolescence: a longitudinal MRI study". Nature neuroscience 2 (10): 861-863.

Z = " If you reflect back upon our own educational training, we have been traditionally taught to master the 3 R's: reading, writing and arithmetic -- the domain and strength of the left brain" -
The Pitek Group, LLC.
Michael P. Pitek, III]

Y + Z = right brain veiled, = separates from god because the god image in man is veiled.

So Jesus knew the way to get back in "Gods graces" by restoring the kingdom, the right hemisphere after the tree of knowledge silenced it.

[Luke 17:33 ..; and whosoever shall lose his life(mindfully) shall (unveil right hemisphere, the god image in man)preserve it.]
[Mark 8:34 ...., he said unto them, Whosoever will come after me, let him deny himself, and take up his cross, and follow me.] =
Get into a situation where the hypothalamus gives one the shadow of death signal and then [lose your life mindfully/ deny yourself]
Jesus was the Lord or the master of the house, house being the mind, he had a sound mind, his house or mind was built upon the a rock because it was sound, he was known as the Lord of Logos ; logos means logic

The truth. what is the truth?

153

This [reading, writing and arithmetic -- the domain and strength of the left brain"] favors left brain so much and when taught to the little ones, it separates them from the god image in man right brain, and they fall from grace.

The light.

What is the light? Right brain. It has intuition (the soul) and is very quick random access processing relative to the quick and the dead and it has complexity and also lots of ambiguity

Ambiguity is why Jesus had moments of Doubt.

So Jesus was the way to truth and the light, he was a good shepherd, if people listened to them and applied the remedy they could restore their mind to a sound state after they got the education, ate off the tree of knowledge.

So Zacharias knew the remedy:

[Luke 1:13 But the angel said unto him, Fear not, Zacharias:] Just like Abraham did [Genesis 15:1 ¶After these things the word of the LORD came unto Abram in a vision, saying, Fear not]

Zacharias told the remedy to his son who was born of a miracle birth (to a sterile Elizabeth) , and his son John the Baptist applied the fear not remedy and came up with his own version, a water version of the fear not remedy, one is dunked under water to the hypothalamus to give the death signal and then one denies their self or fears not.

He assist Jesus with the remedy.

[Mark 1:10 And straightway coming up out of the water, he saw the heavens opened, and the Spirit like a dove descending upon him:]

Heavens opened up = right brain traits were restored

Then Jesus came up with this version of the fear not remedy

[Luke 17:33 ..; and whosoever shall lose his life(mindfully) shall (unveil right hemisphere, the god image in man)preserve it.]

[Mark 8:34 ...., he said unto them, Whosoever will come after me, let him deny himself, and take up his cross, and follow me.]

And Jesus was very good at explaining it to the common people and the ruler scribes heard about Jesus and they had to find a way to get rid of him.

[Matthew 7:29 For he taught them as one having authority, and not as the [scribes.] Matthew 9:3 And, behold, certain of the [scribes] said within themselves, This man blasphemeth.]

154

[Matthew 20:18 Behold, we go up to Jerusalem; and the Son of man shall be betrayed unto the chief priests and unto the [scribes], and they shall condemn him to death,] [Matthew 23:34 Wherefore, behold, I send unto you prophets, and wise men, and [scribes]: and some of them ye shall kill and crucify; and some of them shall ye scourge in your synagogues, and persecute them from city to city:]

[Mark 1:22 And they were astonished at his doctrine: for he taught them as one that had authority, and not as the scribes.]
Why was Jesus' doctrine not as the scribes? Because the scribes were people who got the education and did not apply the remedy and thus were of unsound mind.
[Mark 11:18 And the (common)scribes and chief priests(scribes) heard it, and sought how they might destroy him: for they feared him(a symptom one has not applied the remedy(fear), because all the people was astonished at his doctrine.]
They were afraid because Jesus was explaining flawlessly why the tree of knowledge was mentally hindering everyone.
Once the right hemisphere pattern detection is veiled or hindered by the written education, very obvious correlations in the species collective knowledge becomes undetectable.

4/27/2010 12:53:37 PM – These are some aspects a person can expect once they apply the remedy after they get warmed up a bit. Much less eating of food because a sound mind needs less food. Extreme creativity and ideas at all time, essentially one becomes an "ah ha" sensation. Stress levels are gone and that includes anxiety because one is in the now or the machine state. Sense of humor greatly improves due to the extreme pattern detection aspect of right brain, one makes some very funny observations. Any kinds of psychological medicine perhaps are no longer required because mentally one is essentially always in neutral. One becomes very cerebral and many material desires thus take a back seat. Any addictions are easy to overcome because the addiction thoughts pass very swiftly due to the random access right brain thought patterns. Sense of fatigue is greatly reduced. Sense of time is gone. You "see" things more clearly because you restore the full power of your intuition, pattern detection, ambiguity, and complexity to your perception.

Cognition: knowledge acquired through reasoning, intuition, or perception.

Reverse things applications:

The scribers celebrate the birth of the lights in the season of death and the death of the lights in the season of birth.

Death = Life; Life = Death

The scribes believe written education taught to young children is [Genesis 3:6 ,.. desired to make one(a child) wise.] on an absolute scale.

In reality all that left brain favoring education hinders or veils right hemisphere traits and so in fact does not make one wise it makes one stupid.

Stupid: regarded as showing a lack of intelligence, perception, or common sense.

Sense relative to veiling right brain intuition, pattern detection, complexity, lightning fast random access processing, creativity and thus hinders one's ability to adapt and thus puts one at a disadvantage or in a position of suffering. These are symptoms the scribes are in an alternate perception dimension as a result of the education and thus the scribes out of touch with reality or the absolute perception dimension and is why it is wise if they attempt to apply the remedy. The scribes celebrate the birth of the light in the season of death. Wisdom is not taught for it is a symptom of a sound mind, relative to lateralization.

Every being is doing the best they can based on their perception, understanding, intuition and cognitive ability. Perceptions of victory are lined with delusional ideas of peace; Purpose abhors victory and mocks peace.- 4/27/2010 1:22:13 PM